JÜRGEN SAID TO ME

JÜRGEN SAID TO ME

JÜRGEN **KLOPP**, **LIVERPOOL** AND THE **REMAKING** OF A CITY

DAN MORGAN

First published by Pitch Publishing, 2024
Reprinted 2024
3

Pitch Publishing
9 Donnington Park,
85 Birdham Road,
Chichester,
West Sussex,
PO20 7AJ
www.pitchpublishing.co.uk
info@pitchpublishing.co.uk

© 2024, Daniel Morgan

Every effort has been made to trace the copyright. Any oversight will be rectified in future editions at the earliest opportunity by the publisher.

All rights reserved. No part of this book may be reproduced, sold or utilised in any form or transmitted in any form or by any means, electronic or mechanical, including photocopying, recording or by any information storage and retrieval system, without prior permission in writing from the Publisher.

A CIP catalogue record is available for this book from the British Library.

ISBN 978 1 80150 923 7

Typesetting and origination by Pitch Publishing
Printed and bound in India by Manipal Technologies Limited

Contents

Acknowledgements 6
Prologue 7

Part 1: Change 13
  1. Key to the City 15
  2. UFOs and Loneliness 28
  3. Enough is Enough 46
  4. This is Football 55

Part 2: Inclusion 67
  5. The Liverpool Model 69
  6. If You're Alone, You're Weaker than the Unit 77
  7. If it's Good Enough for You, it's Good Enough for Me . 84
  8. 'Ello, 'Ello 93

Part 3: Champions 103
  9. Our Year 105
  10. The Hurt 117
  11. Tell the World 135

Part 4: Alone 145
  12. An Extremely Shitty Situation 147
  13. Pie in the L4 Sky 167

Part 5: Evolution 185
  14. I Feel Fine 187
  15. Liverpool 2.0 206

Epilogue 220

Acknowledgements

With special thanks to Enis Yucekoralp, Matt Longley and Emerson Leese.

Prologue

*'This club means everything to the people.
So, it's our job to show it means absolutely
everything to us as well.'*

Jürgen Klopp

FRIDAYS IN Liverpool are a hive of mischief and possibility. Early darts have usually been planned or pulled off. Pubs, bars and restaurants fill up. Stag and hen parties flood the Concert Square area of the city centre. The plumes of vape and shisha smoke, cocktailed with sharpening alcohol, tinge the early-evening air. As ever, there's always the purity of the Mersey nearby to offer riverside serenity.

Things are happening: tradition and innovation collide. A copy of *The Echo* – Liverpool's local newspaper – can still be seen rolled into pockets or spread across taxi windscreens. Most people now prefer the transcendence of their phone screens: the incessant head down on the commute after a week of it. All the while, an idyllic backdrop of one of the most fascinating cities on earth remains eternally beautiful in every light.

There's car-sick gridlock on The Strand. Pedestrian shoppers in Liverpool One and Beatlemaniacs from far and wide exploring Matthew Street. A city that caters to so many different desires waits in its own wings. It's partly what attracts regular events such as the Aintree races and those more standalone such as the Eurovision Song Contest. It's a city intertwined with feeling and fuelled by it, and one that demands its status.

On this particular Friday I made my regular commute home from work in Greater Manchester along the Dock Road and its parallel lineage with districts such as Crosby, Litherland and Bootle. The reek of oil pins itself to the back of your throat; the patient wasteland on the shorelines promising a strange sense of nostalgia.

Stories of union leadership within the fraternity of Liverpool's dockworkers in the 1960s and 70s have been passed down to me since birth. The city believes in the rights and agency of the worker. It empowers their ability to be changemakers. The willingness to go from factory line to picket line has never been too far removed as a result.

Between 1995 and 1998 the city's dockworkers engaged in one of the most high-profile cases of striking in recent years. The dockers' standoff against their employers, Mersey Docks and Harbour Company, and Torside Ltd, gained public support from the likes of Robbie Fowler and Noel Gallagher.

Deindustrialisation was catastrophic to Liverpool's port status in the late 1970s onwards, yet it remains a thriving gateway for trade. Towering cranes bow their heads, while resting ships lay dormant, dreaming of Belize, Costa Rica and Guatemala as I drive past. They remind me this was once the only glimpse into a world unknown; when a vessel entered the city, it brought with it a wave of ethnicity, diversity and character.

As I pass through County Road and its perennial affiliation to Everton Football Club, I'm reminded how Liverpool FC was once a breakaway of Merseyside's blue contingent. A new club, spun off across Stanley Park and set up with new divisions in a concrete utopia. I often wonder whether the bitterness and infighting, spawned when John Houlding broke away to realise his new vision on Anfield Road in 1892, have returned in another guise. But somehow it almost feels like the current, increasing unpleasantness around the Merseyside derby still links back to those older origins, rather than its recent history.

PROLOGUE

The familiar drive on to Scotland Road yields a hardened landscape steeped in character. It wears its previous riches heavily and its current struggles brazenly. 'Scottie', as it's known locally, is populated by enduring fables. Usually it's a story that relies on a man who knew a man who also knew a man who usually owned a pub as its leading protagonist.

At the height of Liverpool's early 19th-century port trade, Scotland Road was said to have the greatest number of pubs in Europe on one single stretch of road. I don't know the exact number, but sit in any existing watering hole for long enough and the names will be reeled off. The Throstles Nest, The Jamaica, Lulu's (technically Westminster Road, but a favourite on the basis that it's actually named Leigh Arms) and The Honky Tonk will all get a mention. As will all the stories about sailors who would come to see Scottie as their own shore-leave survival contest.

Weather-battered seafarers would take to the road with the intention of having a beer in every establishment over the course of one night. Nobody was ever said to have completed the task. The unlucky contestant would usually end up greeting the dawn in the doorway of the place where they'd eventually succumbed.

* * *

This Friday was in 2015. It was during a time when the city of Liverpool felt gripped by a heightened sense of anticipation in the face of central government austerity under the Conservative Party (something that was far from unfamiliar to its people). The impact of a vote to leave the European Union had not yet been enforced on a place that had benefited greatly from its individual funding schemes.

Creativity could easily be found in places such as the Baltic Triangle – a former wasteland on the south side of the city centre – which had transformed into an urban patchwork for those seeking cheap rents and alternative communities. Arts and theatre were producing independent and culturally rich offerings. Places such as Duke Street were given a new lease of life, and a massive redevelopment of the Royal Liverpool University Hospital was close to completion. However, this would ultimately grind to a halt and end in administrative failure on the part of the developer. A similar tale for the Chinatown region of the city occurred soon after. This left a huge hole of wasteland dressed in billboards, projecting a metropolis that would never arrive.

In many ways, this book is about feeling. People often label nostalgia as an unhealthy dwelling on past events. Yet nostalgia has become a focus of enquiry in university departments across the globe; a whole new field of academic study that takes in sociology and political science as well as psychology. Nostalgia has been increasingly proven to have a positive impact on things such as social isolation and empathy.

You remember a time based on a feeling. You associate yourself with an occasion because of euphoria, sadness or resolve. It could be viewed as morose, but years become reduced to a flickering second: an afterthought that we instantly seek solace in when recollecting the proverbial 'good times'.

In the end we're perhaps only as relevant as the songs we've loved, nights out we've had or the matches we've won. It's those that leave us wanting new memories – the next win, another night. I've learned through writing this book that this is something to embrace. That this was the time of our lives.

As someone who had just bought their first home on the outskirts of town the summer before, this time would go down as the one of the moments I felt fully exposed to a city I love. I'd shown myself snippets of it in the previous 27 years, but it was only now that I'd really arrived at that place.

There was an overwhelming surge of energy present around me. Liverpool always feels on the cusp of something. Adventure is never far away. From Bootle to Bogotá, Garston to Glastonbury, Scousers will always find the party.

PROLOGUE

Later that evening I went to meet some friends for dinner on Lodge Lane. Liverpool 8 has breakout streets that bustle with worldly influence in a way no other corner of the city manages – and 'Lodgey' or 'The Lane' is its hub.

Making my way through town that night was fairly routine. The Georgian hallmarks of Rodney Street were as poorly lit and eerie as local occult experts would have you believe. The sloped ascent up Hardman Street provided its usual odyssey of nightlife action. There, I was drawn to a small crowd in a seating area outside The Old Blind School, a bar and restaurant now named The Florist.

I was stopped at the traffic lights. There wasn't much happening. But then something piqued my interest about this gathering: a group on a night out taking a picture with someone seemingly sat having a beer, too hidden to make out. Their excitement was bubbling up.

Town had all its usual razzmatazz. Liverpool is a night out done properly. But this felt different. The usual flaunting of dress code was tuned to a different pitch: the rollers were in and the heels were higher than normal. My feeling of anticipation on this day was notably heightened. I'd felt it from a rival city all day long, and now I was consumed by it like a nauseating perfume.

After arriving home, I quickly scanned social media for evidence of the commotion. There, circulating wildly, were the pictures of the scene I'd witnessed sat stationary at the red light earlier.

The figure in the cap I couldn't make out was Jürgen Norbert Klopp – and, as of that day, he was the manager of Liverpool Football Club.

Ultimately, this book tells the story of one man's impact on a place in time. It will be told from people who experienced it both directly and indirectly: everyday people, the type who Klopp would come to love, challenge and require in equal measure.

JÜRGEN SAID TO ME

As he knows only too well, a place is truly defined by its people. In Liverpool, he inherited a unique blend of character and resolve. A place awoken by a man who helped them his way, the Liverpool way.

Part 1

Change

Chapter 1

Key to the City

IT'S IMPOSSIBLE to mention Liverpool without factoring in its football clubs or musical influence. They run through it like the snaking and arching road of Queens Drive, which pierces the city from north to south. These forces carry the city culturally and communally and shape new generations of men and women on their journey: from The Cavern to The State, from Anfield to Goodison Park.

You can look beyond the stadiums, museums and Matthew Street sentimentality to feel it. Walk past any karaoke pub – of which there are many – and The Beatles will likely be blurring from within. The odds of them being covered well are lower, but you'd be a fool to quibble about quality when 'Norwegian Wood' is emanating from Coopers Bar at 11am.

Listen to any conversation on a walk around the place and football won't be far away. In the years that preceded Klopp's arrival, Liverpool had become a topic of frustration among its own. A team managed by Brendan Rodgers regressed quite spectacularly following the whirlwind Premier League title charge of 2013/14. It led to another sense of false dawns and distant paths to glory at home and abroad. The mood was one of disillusionment; not just on the pitch, but also towards Liverpool's American owners, Fenway Sports Group (FSG), and their general running of the club.

Rodgers's era was marred by squabble and disagreement relating to the club's infamous transfer committee, and a frustration around not punching its weight as a football powerhouse. The club hadn't had anywhere near the amount of success it demands. Without trophies it's impossible to envisage Liverpool as a true representation of its supporters and city. It's been the minimum requirement since Bill Shankly promised to make the club a 'bastion of invincibility' from 1959 to 1974.

The failed and almost fatal era of Tom Hicks and George Gillett's ownership from 2007–2010 – in which John W. Henry's 11th-hour, High Court ownership battle ensured he could take the reins at Anfield – had left the club with no identifiable path to future success. A new stadium on Stanley Park was all but dead as a concept – the idea of Anfield expansion was now the preferred route. But Liverpool had, and still have, work to do on this front.

Anfield is a deprived area, and the club has, at times, been far from a perfect neighbour. From certain quarters there was a sense the club didn't care about the community. This led to a wider sense of disassociation from an enterprise so pivotal and inescapable to local lives.

Klopp came into a club that, for an entire generation, had been united with its collective supporter base in brief spurts and fleeting moments, only for fragmentation to take hold once again.

Rafael Benítez had at least generated a sense of unity strong enough to galvanise his early years between 2004 and 2007. Yet the Spaniard – for all his goodwill and intention – was so deep in the trenches of Hicks's and Gillett's subterfuge that he soon became battle-worn by a job that has come to overwhelm and consume so many.

In my supporting Liverpool life, the period of pre-Klopp success that sticks out most was Gérard Houllier's 2000/01 season when Liverpool went on to win a treble of Worthington, FA and UEFA Cups, as well as qualifying for the Champions League via a third-place finish. I witnessed an incredibly resolute team – one Jamie Carragher cites as the best he played in – coupled with an equally resolute style.

Houllier built his team on discipline and tactical frugality. To win, they had to be harder than any other to break down. That often drew criticism whenever stalemates were played out, or when his team diced with the odds to eventually prosper.

There was a generation of supporters steadily giving way to another who hadn't experienced what many had known to be 'the Liverpool way' – a team that not only wins but represents values and understands what's required. A team that's an embodiment of its city.

Houllier's team, like Benítez's, had a limited shelf life. It felt like they'd hit their peak early, and the squad was troubled by a boom-and-bust element.

Until 2015 and Klopp's arrival, the club was a supine enterprise that should have been so much more. That it wasn't hurt people and impacted its overall energy. Liverpool is a global footballing superpower in the heartland of what feels like a small communal village: the city knows the business of everything and everyone. Behaviours are a group endeavour.

It's only now that I've left Liverpool for the first time in my life that I feel able to both assess and appreciate its complexity. Its aesthetic beauty is unquestionable, and, as avid Mancunian Terry Christian admitted on an LFCTV documentary: 'You lot got the prettier city.' It's the phantasmagoria that makes me stomach-churningly miss home. It's the whispering complexities of the place that leave me still needing more time away to decompress and fully understand it.

Being somewhere else leaves me with a need to retrain. I no longer associate a car horn with someone I know making an overt attempt to say hello. Taxi drivers have no desire for interaction from menial destination queries to the question of 'Red or Blue', which will define the comfort of your remaining journey. No longer can I walk into The Crocodile pub on Harringdon Street, on a Sunday football team night out, and find at least five people I've either played with or against, who will tell me how they know someone who knows someone who knows a friend of mine or a family member.

Liverpool is a heaving metropolis of unfinished cycle lanes and unnecessary roadworks. Yet it will somehow still allow you to be anywhere in 20 minutes. It's an inner-city struggle paired with stunning waterfront architecture. It's colloquialisms and quick wordplay for purposes of laughs, and the constant evading of law enforcement's prying eyes and ears.

People supporting the club from outside Liverpool often reference feelings of alienation along with incredible warmth. Supporters inside the city will tell you they feel less valued than those outside. To unite these elements seems at times so impossible that most managers don't bother trying. The only way is to show that you understand that people will ultimately invest in what they see with equal measure. But doing this with feeling is usually of no interest or importance, or, worse still, fabricated.

What makes Klopp the person who somehow knitted so many complicated fractions together? A man born under Germany's post-war cloud in the Swabian town of Glatten, who had no affiliation or real understanding of Liverpool's inner workings.

Jürgen was the son of Elisabeth and Norbert Klopp – the latter a professional goalkeeper and salesman with a passion for sport in all forms, notably football, tennis and boxing. Elisabeth had previously given birth to two daughters: Stefanie and Isolde. To the relief of all, Jürgen was the last child to come along, but Norbert felt he could transmit his fatherly love and desire for sporting competition into a boy who might go on to become a professional footballer as he was.

Klopp would later describe how his father would take him running daily in all terrains. He would let Jürgen run the perimeter of a football field before eventually taking him over; that is, until Norbert could no longer catch up to his protégé's improved stamina.

An early start into the competitive and physical demands of elite sport led Jürgen to a modest playing career. He later described himself as having a 'fourth division talent with a first division brain'. In 1990 his journey eventually took him to Mainz 05 under the guidance of the man Klopp considers his greatest sporting influence, Wolfgang Frank. The introspective coach would go on to revolutionise German football's long-held belief that success was built on the employment of a sweeper system by demolishing it and replacing it with a high-pressing flat back four.

Frank coupled this tactical iconoclasm with running. He was an advocate of finding marginal gains that made his players fitter. He felt he could marry this with a style of play based on Arrigo Sacchi's AC Milan that would later be described by Mainz CEO Christian Heidel as 'ball orientated zonal marking'.

At first his players struggled to adapt. Fans raged in the stands at how much space they were seeing being vacated in front of them. They feared that an opposition midfielder could run through them easily, or a press could be bypassed by a long ball over the top of the defence to leave the striker with a free run on goal. None of this aligned with Germany's conservative approach that had won them three World Cups.

Frank's principles – shifting opposing players into positions where they weren't allowed space and time, combined with and regaining possession high up the pitch – were eventually beginning to show on the pitch. The modest outfit went from relegation certainties in the eyes of the German media to unlikely promotion contenders by the winter break of 1997.

If Frank's blueprint is a familiar one to Liverpool supporters, his character was definitely what set him apart from Klopp. Described as having a schoolteacher persona, Frank's innate attention to detail meant he took setbacks and defeats very badly. In two stints at Mainz, he left abruptly after a run of bad results that were far from catastrophic. His legacy and mark had already been left on Klopp, who had completed a degree in sports science in 1995 while keeping a keen and sometimes critical eye on coaches and their systems post-Frank.

It was when Heidel and Mainz took the decision to gamble on Klopp, following the dismissal of Eckhard Krautzun early in the 2000/01 season, that everyone realised they'd stumbled on something. Heidel knew he had a squad of players that understood each other and the system. He believed the players could coach themselves; all they needed was someone at the helm with their name above the door. He decided that would be the veteran squad member Klopp (much to the amusement of the journalists who attended the press conference that unveiled him). 'The whole table roared with laughter. They cracked up,' Heidel stated in Raphael Honigstein's 2017 book *Klopp: Bring the Noise*.

Klopp steered Mainz to safety in Germany's second tier at the end of 2001. He was adamant that the greatest lesson of all, even in his managerial infancy, was that he needed passion and buy-in from everyone at the club to push forward. Suddenly, people were taking Klopp the manager deadly serious.

Klopp made an invisible contract with players and supporters alike. He would lay down the gauntlet of giving everything, in return for receiving just that. He was rewarded with a two-year deal with the aim of making 'little old Mainz' a Bundesliga club.

Two seasons of devastating last-gasp setbacks would see them miss out on promotion in a manner that was enough to break anyone. Yet Klopp, operating on a shoestring budget and with a provincial city modestly offering its backing, remained defiantly unmovable.

'We will pick ourselves up,' he was quoted as saying. 'We are still young, nobody has to give up just yet. We're determined to do so much more for the city and our fans. I know that people say: "Mainz will never do it." But they have a problem. We'll be back. Anyone who writes us off is making a serious mistake,' he vowed.

Consecutive seasons of missing out on taking Mainz to the Promised Land by a single goal and a single point meant promotion the season after. A modest tally of 54 points was enough to finish third. The city was in full party mode, led by a man who always knew and appreciated when the time to enjoy life with a beer was upon him.

Mainz finished their first-ever Bundesliga season in 11th place, and the brand and identity of Klopp's aggressive football never wavered. Mainz were doing things their way – the only way they knew how under Klopp – and it was reaping benefits. The supporters were pinching themselves that summer, after the team had inadvertently qualified for the UEFA Cup by way of Fair Play rankings. It would prove to be a blessing and a curse, with extra exertion hugely affecting the domestic form in 2005/06.

Although the European campaign was short-lived, Mainz eventually regrouped in the league to match their 11th-place finish of the previous season. Klopp had signed a two-year extension in that time. To Heidel and the board he was the single-most important asset the club had possessed in their history.

The next season brought the club crashing down to earth. A devastating start to the campaign left them with too great a mountain to climb. After 102 intoxicating matches in the top flight, FSV descended back into the second tier of German football.

Klopp was unable to regain promotion in 2007/08, missing out once again on the final day to TSG 1899 Hoffenheim. Throughout the season, advances from other clubs had come in, including FC Bayern Munich, but nothing had materialised. Had Mainz won promotion, Klopp had stated he would commit to a new deal. But by that time a new club was in conversation with Weidel to make him their coach. It was, like every step in Klopp's managerial career, the perfect move at the perfect time.

The hiring of Klopp at a flailing Borussia Dortmund in 2008 was viewed by many as a gamble. Perhaps none more so than the club's ultras. The most passionate members of its supporter base assumed that hiring a manager from a club like Mainz was unambitious and wouldn't raise them from their perpetual state of slumber. They were quickly won over by Klopp, who met them with his wife Ulla to understand the club and its fans more. He talked, laughed and played cards with the group until, like most who encounter him, they were eating out of his hands.

If the supporters were excited by Klopp the man, they would soon see that the principles he'd learned from Frank were becoming even more defined. But the philosophy would take time and result in some major setbacks and questions about his credentials.

Klopp stood by his gegenpressing strategy, insisting to his players that it wasn't about retreating when they lost the ball; instead, they should surge forward in a buzz of yellow and black to win it back immediately. Everything had to be in unison or it wouldn't work. If a player setting the press missed, the next one had to be ready to join instinctively by being in the right position.

The replacement of players such as Croatian Mladen Petrić – the club's leading scorer from the previous season – raised eyebrows, but he was insistent some were not right for the system. Instead, faith was placed in a 19-year-old centre-back partnership of Neven Subotić and Mats Hummels, initially on loan from Bayern. Klopp also brought in players such as Mohamed Zidan, who he'd worked with at Mainz, and tireless forward Lucas Barrios.

But it was the €4.25m signing of Robert Lewandowski from Lech Poznań in 2010 that would go down in history. He would go on to score 103 goals in 74 matches, 25 of which proved to be match-winning strikes.

Lewandowski was part of a machine-like force of yellow that ripped through the Bundesliga and catapulted Dortmund to the league title in 2010/11 and 2011/12. The famous Yellow

Wall in the Signal Iduna Park was shaken to its foundations by the sheer ecstasy of such an unthinkable achievement.

Klopp had built a formula, for players who were fitter, smarter and too tactically sharp for anyone to match. It had taken three years of disciplined strategic implementation coupled with astute plays in the transfer market from Sporting Director Michael Zorc for things to fully click into place.

Consecutive Bundesliga titles were complemented by a 5-2 final win in the DFB-Pokal over Bayern Munich at the Olympic Stadium. The Bavarians were embarrassed, with Bayern CEO Karl-Heinz Rummenigge describing every goal like a 'slap in the face'. Klopp, on the other hand, had described the win as 'the most extraordinary moment in [Dortmund] history'.

That was enough for a Munich call to arms. They flexed their football muscles with sinewing plagiarism. Not only did Bayern imitate a style of high-energy pressing from the front line, but they did it with a more expensively assembled squad. Those squad additions included targeting Dortmund's key assets. On the eve of a Champions League semi-final with Real Madrid in 2013, news broke that academy graduate, wunderkind and true Dortmunder Mario Götze was joining Bayern after they'd triggered a release clause in his contract. That was followed swiftly by increasing talk that Lewandowski was bound for the Allianz Arena that summer. Klopp had already had to deal with setbacks of losing Shinji Kagawa and Nuri Şahin, but the potential loss of Götze and Lewandowski would be seen as catastrophic.

Dortmund rallied and ran all over José Mourinho's Real Madrid to set up a Der Klassiker final with Bayern at Wembley. A slender 2-1 defeat would once again contribute to Klopp's modesty and awareness that football can throw you miracles and heartbreak in equal measure. Klopp reiterated his belief that everything is about the next 90 minutes, and in every one of those minutes you have to fight with your life, or you'll earn nothing.

After back-to-back titles, Klopp's Dortmund would twice finish as runners-up to Pep Guardiola's new-look Bayern. Dortmund continued to lose key players via a transfer strategy that reaffirmed their place in the food chain: always one rung below their biggest German counterparts and other global superclubs.

When the domestic winter break arrived in 2014/15, Dortmund were languishing in the lower half of the table thanks to a horrendous injury run and disrupted pre-season – one of the things Klopp strives to avoid ahead of every campaign. They would eventually finish seventh but, a year after Klopp had signed a new deal, he knew it was time to depart.

Within that time he held talks with Edward Woodward and Manchester United after David Moyes's ill-fated run as manager had ended. Woodward tried to sell United as 'an adult version of Disneyland', completely misreading both the room and person he was wooing. Klopp turned United down, but a glimpse of his next destination had come in the summer of 2014, when he brought Dortmund to Anfield for a friendly. Laying out his biggest smile and bringing his booming laugh, he followed tradition and touched the 'This is Anfield' sign when leaving the tunnel. Klopp had Liverpool's attention and vice versa.

When Liverpool contacted Klopp's agent, Marc Kosicke, due diligence was conducted. Klopp met with FSG in New York and provided a dossier on his playing style and all other factors he deemed imperative to success. Everything centred on uniting the club to push the team forward.

Klopp had to reignite the spark of a collective supporter base that had dwindled after too many false starts and fracturing elements. The club still had an identity, but this was often its downfall: it relied on a vision of itself no longer relevant to the meandering outfit it had become.

On the day Klopp was appointed manager, 8 October 2015, his press conference was remembered for soundbites about him being 'the normal one', and how we had to turn 'doubters to believers'. There was, however, a more nuanced insight into his workings and the impact he would have on a place when asked about how it felt to be manager of the club: 'It's not important what people said when you come in, but what they say when you leave. If we want, this could be a special day. We can start in a very difficult league and in a special Liverpool way we can be successful. If we sit here in four years, I think we win a title, I'm pretty sure.'

He also made reference to the weight of Liverpool's history being somewhat burdensome, stating that carrying history 'like a backpack' wouldn't be allowed – another sign he was willing to be bold in challenging the club's supporters. This was Klopp laying a marker for meeting halfway. In that moment he didn't care about image. What mattered was showing the people his team would give everything in terms of hard work, representation and values.

It's important to remember how football was being consumed and digested around this time. The emergence of more accessible fan engagement meant that there was always a counter-narrative to be found. Platforms were, and remain, optional to engage with, but they fast became the go-to place for the instant reaction and content we crave. Even the most joyous of days like Klopp's arrival can be sullied by the persecution and dissenting voice from the faceless online.

Social media now creates far more instant pressure than any of the tabloid press hounds that dominated previous decades. There's no longer outrage and opinion saved cynically for morning print. There was also the rise of more fan media and platforms, which allowed people to access relatable insight on a topic they were already routinely invested in.

It's what led to my own eventual contribution on *The Anfield Wrap*, to me changing careers and inevitably to this book. I'd often felt there was a place for me in this field, and Klopp to Liverpool elevated that to another level because of my interest in him as a person.

I instantly thought of this, and him, as being different. I was witnessing something beyond the semantics of performances and results. More fascinating was the sense of feeling a shift in an entire city. Klopp had lit the pyrotechnics and Liverpool was a smoking red blaze.

What followed was a journey so mesmeric and inspiring most would have struggled to believe. It has captured togetherness, human will, social impact and a place in time so perfectly that it feels like we've borne witness to an astrological phenomenon.

Klopp has become more than the leading figure of footballing operations at a sporting institution. He has become a figurehead for matters relating to everyday life and society, to the point that the world of politics is now calling for him to use his skillset there.

At the heart of this lies a city of unbreakable character, despite being tested to its limit. Liverpool is steeped in tradition and trauma. It will give you its heart, but don't dare cast an envious glance elsewhere. It's the best dressed, most outspoken and, at times, most confusing place on the planet, but its beauty and authenticity can't be equalled. It's a city that most of the time deserves better than its lot from local and central government, yet still finds a way to look after itself.

Klopp did and does understand all of this. On Wednesday, 2 November 2022, at a special ceremony held at Liverpool Town Hall, he was awarded the Freedom of the City of Liverpool, an honour granted to individuals to recognise exceptional services to the city. In his interview with the club when announcing his departure, he admitted he didn't know such an honour existed. When accepting the accolade, he stated:

> Over the years you realise that the Scouse people and us as a family have a lot of things in common. We care about similar things, have similar political views and we like to be very open, that's how it is. All people

around me, my friends and family, see more of the city than I do, and I hear that they enjoy it exactly because of that; because people are really open, nice, kind and friendly. That's what I want to be as well.

Chapter 2

UFOs and Loneliness

LIVERPOOL'S SKYLINE will match most for beauty. The outline of its Liver Building clock face and two cathedrals – Anglican and Metropolitan – will look equally stunning from Knowsley's East Lancashire Road or Runcorn bridge. For those who were born there, those who have adopted it as their home and the many passing through, it drenches you in such profound sentiment that you feel compelled to know its story.

Most city skylines offer a nod to its character. New York has Manhattan, Seattle the Space Needle, and Berlin the Fernsehturm. For Liverpool it is St Johns Beacon (or the Radio City Tower as it became known). A 138-metre-high, free-standing building at the heart of the city centre built in 1969 as a revolving five-star luxury restaurant. The structure has been described in local quarters as a 'white elephant'. Others reference its resemblance to an extraterrestrial object hovering over those below.

The original restaurant was closed in 1979 due to health and safety concerns. It would reopen in other guises, including a 'Buck Rogers' space-themed eatery in 1983, but it soon closed again due to lack of business.

In August 2000 it eventually became the home of Radio City 96.7 and Magic 1548 – a local broadcast station then owned by Emap Radio.

The tower operates on two levels only; the first is filled with recording studios and the second as offices. The tower no longer rotates (thankfully for those who are employed there) but is renowned for swaying in high winds, which Liverpool is never shy of.

By the time Klopp arrived at Liverpool in 2015, the station (then owned by Bauer Media) had expanded its network to also include sister stations Radio City 2 and Radio City Talk. City Talk was a staple of excellent local interest content, which covered news, local democracy issues, mental health and sport incredibly well. If you wanted a comprehensive build-up to a major event in the city such as the Aintree Grand National, or a well-informed conversation about topics such as knife crime on Merseyside, City Talk was essential listening.

For employees and contributors, there was no better place to work. Its panoramic views offered a watchful eye over a bustling metropolis. It was a guardian to those below, responsible for telling Liverpool's story in various ways, especially through football.

I was lucky enough to contribute to City Talk's impeccable broadcasting for around two years prior to the Covid-19 pandemic. My slot was alongside David Fehily, a true Evertonian of north Liverpool heritage with wonderful heart and resolve. We would chew over matters relating to Merseyside football every Monday for an hour at 5pm, guided by Matt Jones, who presented and produced several sports shows over the final years of City Talk's broadcast.

Jones's demeanour was always relaxed. If he wasn't talking football, he would invariably be eyeballing a cricket score from around the globe on his monitor. Jones and his producer Matt Houghton were both Tranmere Rovers supporters, which worked perfectly in remaining neutral to the incessant Liverpool and Everton rhetoric that dominated the airwaves.

City Talk ceased broadcasting in May 2020, with the coronavirus pandemic providing too much of a challenge to its existence. This was a great loss to me, but more importantly to the city. It was a true staple of Liverpool identity. Gladly, when the idea of contributing to this project came up, Jones had no hesitation in reminiscing about his time there:

> It was a real thrill to be a small part of the Radio City and Radio City Talk team for seven years. Merseyside is a region like very few across the country. We don't just watch our football teams. We idolise them. As fans, we do everything in our power to make sure our team, be it Liverpool, Everton or Tranmere, gets the result required.
>
> Radio is an incredibly powerful form of media. It's not reliant on your full attention, like a newspaper might be, for you to have a full grasp of the story being told. People tune in and out as they please. Some use it as background noise when working, dipping in and out when their concentration allows. For others it's a familiar and welcome companion.
>
> But that mainly applies to music radio. Speech radio is different. When you're holding an interview, or providing updates from a live sporting event, you have the listeners' full and undivided attention. They are tuning in, avidly, to what you have to say. And for that reason, it was a great privilege to be able to give those listeners the information they wanted to or in many cases didn't want to hear. Transfer sagas, goals, manager departures. We lived them all, and when the big news broke, it was thrilling and exciting, trying to reflect the importance of what was happening by speaking to the biggest footballing names in the city.
>
> You knew that what you were doing was worthwhile, because people wanted it, and you could see it in the listening figures. During the off-season, figures went down, but you could be sure they would jump back up again when August returned. And while you might not always get recognition for it,

or even any reaction whatsoever, there was always special buzz on those big days.

Unfortunately, times have changed. Local commercial radio from a sporting sense has been absolutely destroyed due to the increase in live televised matches and listening figures declining. There's no commentary service anymore, and stations might not even send journalists to matches and press conferences. But back then, Radio City Sport meant something. It was the voice of Merseyside.

City Talk was at the forefront of insight and reaction to Klopp's arrival at Liverpool in October 2015. Its contributors, from fan media to ex-pros, had Liverpool fizzing with anticipation around what could be achieved.

The club had come through a conflicted period of management under Brendan Rodgers before Klopp signed on the dotted line. Rodgers was backed fervently that summer and had been allowed to change his backroom staff, sending out a message of defiance. But football under Rodgers had become stagnant. He'd taken Liverpool on a miraculous journey that almost delivered a Premier League title nobody had anticipated, in 2013/14. In doing so, he'd shown leadership and tactical maturity beyond his years.

After only one full season at the club, Rodgers had moulded something almost perfectly opportunist. He adopted a diamond midfield shape with the waning Steven Gerrard at its base. A four-from-five approach with Philippe Coutinho, Raheem Sterling, Joe Allen and Jordan Henderson then allowed Liverpool the industry and creativity to create some blistering attacking play.

Simon Mignolet had been brought in from Sunderland to replace Pepe Reina – who followed the likes of Maxi Rodriguez and Dirk Kuyt out the door as a result of their ageing profile and bloated contracts. Mamadou Sakho was also brought in, from Paris Saint-Germain (PSG). Liverpool still had problems at full-back. Glen Johnson was kept around, and a mixture of Aly Cissokho and Jon Flanagan was used at left-back.

It was in attack, with Luis Suárez and Daniel Sturridge, where Rodgers really decided to maximise the tools at his disposal. Suárez was banned for the first six matches, but Liverpool won the first three 1-0 before losing two and drawing one. When he returned they caught fire after a dismal 3-1 defeat to Hull City in December. The momentum shifted with a 5-0 demolition job at Tottenham, which left manager André Villas-Boas visibly shocked on the touchline.

Suárez was running amok in attack. Teams couldn't build prolonged periods of pressure on what was an inexperienced back line because they were simply too afraid of leaving room behind.

By April, the title was in Liverpool's grasp – a reality nobody expected to be living. After beating rivals Manchester City at Anfield to go seven points clear with four to play, the incredulous joy was almost tangible. City had two matches in hand, but that elusive victory felt close.

Many rival fractions will still mockingly cite Gerrard's slip against Chelsea as the moment Liverpool lost the title; but many, including Rodgers, knew that when Henderson was given a straight red card for a tired challenge on Samir Nasri in the dying moments against City, the scales had finally tipped against his threadbare squad.

City would go on to prosper in what has become a familiarly frustrating tale during Klopp's tenure. The following summer saw Suárez leave for Barcelona in an outcome many felt was fair. Liverpool were forthright about having Chilean forward Alexis Sánchez as part of that deal, something the player himself was seemingly against. From a point of holding cards, Liverpool lost both Suárez and Sánchez, who went on to join Arsenal. Further frustration came when a deal for highly rated Queens Park Rangers forward Loïc Rémy fell through when his medical showed heart concerns. Rémy then went on to sign for Chelsea.

Liverpool raided Southampton for their captain, Adam Lallana, and centre-back Dejan Lovren. They also added Alberto Moreno (Sevilla), Emre Can (Leverkusen) and Lazar Marković (Benfica), but still hadn't solved their issues in attack.

Divock Origi was signed and then immediately loaned straight back to Lille. The previous summer's experiment on Iago Aspas hadn't worked and he was shipped to Sevilla on loan. Rickie Lambert had been brought in on a wave of sentiment, given his Liverpool roots, and a returning Fabio Borini was making noises about being in Rodgers's plans after a season at Sunderland.

As the window drew to a close, Liverpool had locked themselves into a choice between an ageing Samuel Eto'o and the enigmatic Mario Balotelli. The Italian was signed for around £18m from AC Milan, which felt like a straight punt.

It didn't work. The 2014/15 season was a mess from beginning to end. Liverpool were heavily unbalanced, and, when Sturridge suffered a serious muscle injury in September after being forced into training sprints the day after featuring for Roy Hodgson's England, too much responsibility fell on the shoulders of Sterling and Coutinho.

Rodgers also lost his way by trying to tactically micromanage the team. He shifted mid-season to a 3-5-2 shape with some moderate success, largely due to Sterling's tactical supremacy and the ability to carry the team forward from positions like right wing-back.

The perfect embodiment of a disjointed season came in a 2-1 FA Cup semi-final defeat to Aston Villa at Wembley. Rodgers had tweaked Liverpool's shape three times in the first half, which left most of his players confused as the manager frantically tried to give instructions.

The 6-1 defeat to Stoke City on the final day of the season was among the lowest points in the club's history. The fans had fully turned on Sterling, who had made it clear through his outspoken agent he wanted to leave. Rodgers was ready to cull his trusted backroom staff members, Colin Pascoe and Mike Marsh, to continue on, while residual anger lingered about how Gerrard was bowing out to join LA Galaxy.

Somehow, the Northern Irishman remained in his post, bringing in Sean O'Driscoll and former Liverpool midfielder Gary McAllister to his backroom team. James Milner, Danny Ings and Roberto Firmino were all signed. Rumours swirled about them being players Rodgers was told from above to work with. The one player Rodgers was said to have pushed for, Aston Villa striker Christian Benteke, was eventually brought in for £32.5m.

The following season started indifferently. Wins against Stoke, Bournemouth and Aston Villa were offset by defeats to Manchester United and West Ham, and a draw at home to Norwich City. A steady Europa League start had also contributed to what felt like a state of purgatory for everyone at the club. Identity and any idea as to where this was leading remained absent.

That all changed after a 1-1 draw with Everton in the Merseyside derby on 4 October 2015. Rodgers was sacked by Liverpool that evening and attention immediately turned to Klopp, who was taking a self-imposed break from football following his hugely successful yet emotional tenure at Borussia Dortmund.

Not much was known about his persona at that point. Focus was instead on his brand of 'heavy-metal football', which had become a staple term to describe Dortmund. Liverpool fans could expect to be entertained under the new manager but, beyond that, who Klopp was and what he stood for remained somewhat less clear.

Jones had seen Liverpool managers come and go in his time as a media journalist on Merseyside. He's reported on all manner of topics from boardroom politics to match reports.

But he remembers the feeling being different when it came to Klopp's arrival:

> I think there was just a real deep sense of excitement. It seemed like the possibilities were endless under Klopp. People really bought into what he might bring not just to Liverpool, but to Merseyside in itself.
>
> I remember being sent out to do vox pops and I remember because I hate doing vox pops. I don't know what it is about them, but I just really dislike door-stepping members of the public going about their day. Anyway, my go-to was usually the taxi rank in Williamson Square, because taxi drivers are always willing to speak – and they've always an opinion that sounds good on radio.
>
> After getting a few Evertonians who, needless to say, knocked my request for a quick word back, I remember speaking to several Reds who were just so excited. They knew they'd prised a top-class manager to Anfield, and as I said earlier, the same probably couldn't be said for any of his recent successors. There was an expectation about not what he could achieve, but what he would achieve. There was so much excitement.
>
> The same could be said for the ex-players we spoke to at Radio City Sport who were queuing up to give their opinion on a manager who, from his CV, was a winner. And let's be honest, spare a few who did watch the Bundesliga, most of us knew very little about him other than his CV. But that CV was enough to get minds wandering to dreams of trophies.

It was Klopp's undoubted charisma at his first press conference that drew people in. Most notably, how relaxed he was. He strode around Anfield, tall, tanned and looking well rested in a blazer, pumps and jeans. He very much carried the mantle of a man certain of himself while also giving the impression that if things didn't work out, it wasn't a catastrophe. That, for the first time, felt liberating to many supporters.

His press conference had carried a message of using history and status as a positive instead of 'a weight on your shoulders', as he put it. Most impressively he had an uncanny knack of leaving you feeling like football was only a game, while remaining the single most important thing in life.

Jones was at his first press conference, an unveiling at Anfield, 'already marking it differently to your bog-standard press calling, which back then were held at Melwood', he reveals.

> It seemed like every media outlet in world football was there. The place was jam-packed. Everybody wanted to hear what he had to say. Why had he taken the Liverpool job? What did it mean to him? What did he want to achieve?
>
> The latter question was answered almost immediately. He outlined that he believed Liverpool would win a title within four years of his arrival. He was spot on, given the Champions League arrived in his fourth full season.
>
> I remember sending a tweet from the Radio City Sport Twitter account. 'It's 10 O'Klopp, and Jürgen has arrived at Liverpool', or something along those lines, with an accompanying picture, showing him in a jet-black shirt. He arrived bang on time.

The sense that Klopp could connect with Liverpool off the pitch wasn't lost on anyone, not least the Metro Mayor of the Liverpool City Region, Steve Rotheram. He hails from Kirkby – a Merseyside town in the borough of Knowsley, which is now the location of Liverpool's AXA training complex. A former bricklayer, Rotheram transitioned to local governance and was elected to represent Labour's Fazakerley ward from 2002 to 2011. He also served as the Lord Mayor of Liverpool from 2008 to 2009 and the MP for Liverpool Walton from 2010 to 2017 before he was elected as Metro Mayor.

Alongside Greater Manchester Mayor Andy Burnham, he continues to fight publicly for improvement to the city's transport and infrastructure links, as well as renewing calls for the passing of a Hillsborough Law to ensure legislation is in place to protect those bereaved by public tragedies.

Rotheram makes no secret of his Liverpool-supporting life. He was in Paris for the 2022 Champions League Final. When he sits down for this interview, he recalls what Klopp being announced felt like from beyond a footballing perspective. Liverpool had, perhaps, found the perfect ambassador to lead one of its most prestigious institutions:

> I think his declaration that he was 'the Normal One' really struck a chord with local people. He was humble and had a sense of humour, the sort of personality that people find very endearing in our area, and traits that Scousers are renowned for.
>
> Above all else, it was clear from the moment he started speaking that he understood just how much football meant to people here. He gets the city, he gets the fans, he gets our passion and that's why he's built such a special relationship with the fanbase. To truly succeed as a Liverpool manager, you need that emotional connection. Not every manager has it – but he has it in spades.

Liverpool would soon get a taste of Klopp's impact on the pitch. His first match, a 0-0 draw with Tottenham at White Hart Lane on 17 October 2015, had Adam Lallana collapsing into his manager's arms with exhaustion when substituted. The performance had all the hallmarks of a Liverpool team willing to show fighting qualities.

Klopp had come in with a different slant on spending money than others. Rather than complain about the team he'd inherited, or lament the previous strategy, which now required restructuring, he struck the opposite chord. 'I really like the team. I sometimes feel like the team doesn't like the team. But if I wasn't happy with the squad I wouldn't be here,' he said shortly after his arrival.

Klopp immediately changed how Liverpool were set up, moving Firmino to a more central position and ensuring that Coutinho had enough license to operate by putting legs and industry around him in the form of Can, Milner, Henderson and Lucas Leiva.

There were signs of what could be achieved as early as a 3-1 win away at Chelsea on 31 October, but the lack of squad depth meant that philosophy would have to be held back in place of pragmatism.

After a 3-0 downing at the hands of Watford in December, a dishevelled Klopp was brutally honest in his post-match assessment, noting that 'we lost our minds after the first goal'. Klopp could accept mistakes from players such as goalkeeper Ádám Bogdán (who was never going to form part of his long-term plans), but he couldn't tolerate a poor reaction or a loss of discipline. For Klopp, there is always a chance to put something right during a match.

He would, of course, go on to rebalance the squad's quality with incredible players such as Sadio Mané, Mohamed Salah, Virgil van Dijk and Alisson Becker, but his core principles remained. Those principles led to an alleged pact made between the management and players at the start of each season: you buy into the collective unconditionally or you find a future elsewhere.

For Klopp, this allows for unity on all fronts and for personal gripes, from playing time to salary wrangles, to be left at the door. He demands it because he knows the power of such unity. He said in a 2016 press conference:

> If a player comes to me and says he doesn't feel comfortable and wants to leave because of our style of play or because he can make more money elsewhere, then you always have to start thinking. That's all I can say on this.
>
> Coutinho, Firmino, so many players are very special. You could go through the whole squad. But if a player wants to go to another club, then I'd always be open to it because I don't want to have a player in my squad who doesn't want to be in the squad.
>
> These are problems you don't need during a season. A player is never good enough for you to have to cope with problems like that for an entire year.

His initial home matches weren't producing wins. Worse, there was a feeling inside Anfield that too many people had seen far too much unsuccessful football for too long. People had come to view the match-going experience as a chore. They saw opponents winning inoffensive set pieces as a sign of impending doom. There was a rush to leave the stadium early (which is understandable to a degree, given Anfield's excruciatingly absent transport links and lack of efficiency when it comes to navigating a way in and out of the stadium vicinity).

But it didn't go unnoticed by Klopp, who raised it after a defeat to Crystal Palace at Anfield in only his third match in charge: 'After the goal on 82 minutes, with 12 minutes to go, I saw many people leaving the stadium,' he said post-match. 'I felt pretty alone at this moment. We decide when it is over. Between 82 and 94 [minutes] you can make eight goals if you like.'

The point was far from veiled. He couldn't understand why people left, especially if they left having witnessed a team giving absolutely everything for them.

He knew this had to change on the pitch to see its impact off it. When Divock Origi scored a 96th-minute equaliser against West Bromwich Albion on 13 October 2016, a procession of players hand-in-hand, led by Klopp, took themselves to the Kop and bowed as one in gratification, drawing widespread mockery from media and opposition fans alike.

The point was missed. Klopp wasn't celebrating a draw with Tony Pulis's squad of journeymen on the famous hallowed turf. He was saying thank you to those who remained until the very end and were rewarded with something in return. Nobody gave up that day. It was his imprint slowly taking shape in a manner which others thought was hilarious. The message to the Anfield contingent couldn't have been clearer.

That season continued with Liverpool slowly finding their way. Klopp had found stability with a makeshift 4-2-3-1 system, with Origi leading the line and Firmino dropping into the half-spaces to link play nicely. A 4-0 Merseyside derby win over Everton in April saw his team total 64 touches inside the opposition penalty area; Everton managed just three.

His outfit were starting to look deadly serious. They'd evolved and matured slightly with each passing week, seeing off Manchester United in the Europa League quarter-final en route to the showcase showdown with Sevilla. Both legs of the United tie showed how important momentum would be in the coming seasons.

At Anfield in the first leg, Liverpool were relentless in attack, getting numbers into the box with aggressive running. The visitors couldn't handle them and eventually succumbed to a 2-0 defeat. The second leg had Old Trafford bubbling after an early penalty was converted to put them back in the tie, but a delightful solo effort from Coutinho at the Stretford End killed the affair dead.

The crowning moment of the season would be the blockbuster 4-3 win over Borussia Dortmund at Anfield, a night that would go down as one of the greatest in the history of such an esteemed club. After drawing the first leg 1-1, Liverpool hosted Klopp's former club for the return fixture. Liverpool were blown away by early goals from Henrikh Mkhitaryan and Pierre-Emerick Aubameyang. By the time Liverpool were 3-1 down on the hour mark, the feeling of a required miracle was a common goal.

Coutinho struck from distance on 66 minutes and suddenly the stadium exploded into life, taking its lead from the Kop. When the home team won a corner on 78 minutes, Mats Hummels was trying desperately to instil some calm in his team from the goalmouth. Sakho put Liverpool level from the resulting set piece, and from that moment until Lovren's rise to meet Milner's cross in injury time, Klopp's former employers knew what was coming: 'I remember in an interview, Klopp told me he'd settled for 3-3. He described it as Anfield's goal,' quipped Neil Atkinson, CEO and presenter of *The Anfield Wrap* podcast.

If Dortmund was the football miracle many couldn't believe for weeks and months after, to Klopp it was a sign that loneliness was fast becoming an issue he no longer had in the dying moments of matches. Whether winning, losing or drawing there was a dawning epiphany that the crowd and players could make something happen. Klopp's desire for football by collective consensus was starting to become evident, as was just how different a manager he was from his predecessors.

The need for hero worship has never been far away from Liverpool and its football teams. Both have sought relatability and likability from those in charge. There's a need to understand the club and the place culturally, but that level of understanding is never fully elaborated.

Before Klopp and Rodgers, Liverpool had both Rafael Benítez and the late Gérard Houllier – two very different men with strong personalities that both suited and alienated fractions of the club. Houllier was, in his own way, a revolutionary who modernised Liverpool in line with football's now revered marginal gains approach. He could also play the antagonist, falling out with players such as Robbie Fowler, adored by the Kop, and wanting to eradicate parts of ex-player culture at Anfield, which he viewed as overly critical.

Benítez was someone who was notorious for his lack of affection towards players. He was seen as cold and astute, and despite having most supporters behind him, many grew increasingly frustrated by his stubbornness around substitutions, which were deemed too sideways and lacking in pragmatism.

Both enjoyed their status of terrace adoration. They would meet the chant of their names with applause and appreciation. Why wouldn't they? The respect of the Anfield crowd remains something to strive for across the game. Opposition goalkeepers will get one round of applause when they run to the Kop every match. If they fail to reciprocate, it won't be forgotten.

That's why Klopp's reaction to his name being sung during his early tenure surprised everyone. Unlike Houllier or Benítez emerging from the dugout with a modest hand raised like a post-symphony conductor, Klopp launched into a foul-mouthed tirade against those around him – reminding them in no uncertain terms that their support should lay firmly with the team and helping them win.

This never became confrontational or problematic, just another way of Klopp making tweaks to the mindset of match-going thousands and their generations of habitual behaviours. That action takes courage. Liverpool's is seen as a crowd that's one of the most tribal and partisan around. They pride themselves on an unspoken set of values. A manager calling them out during a match had best be ready to back that up with evidence that another way can work.

Klopp would form a continuous bond with the Kop, which would be marked with his trademark fist-pumps – something most supporters now stay well after the final whistle for. It's another example of him breaking past traditions and doing things his own way. Jones recalls:

> Under Houllier, Manchester United had become the dominant force in this country. That's where the money was and that's where the big players generally went. Liverpool churned out some unbelievable talents from the academy, with Jamie Carragher and Steven Gerrard following in the footsteps of Robbie Fowler and Michael Owen who had already made their debuts.
>
> Houllier relied on them, but also built a team around astute signings such as Dietmar Hamann, Stéphane Henchoz and Sami Hyypiä. They would become the spine of the team for several years to come, but did you really think at the time they were the best players in their position, as good as, say, Freddie Ljungberg, Robert Pires, Patrick Vieira or Sol Campbell at Arsenal, or Jaap Stam, Rio Ferdinand, Paul Scholes or Ryan Giggs at Manchester United?
>
> The same could be said of the early Benítez teams. Xabi Alonso was incredible, so too, at times, the likes of Luis García and Pepe Reina. But other than Gerrard, there wasn't anyone in that team who would truly be considered world-class, and by that I mean would they have got in every other team in the club game?
>
> Both managers signed industrious players such as Steve Finnan, Milan Baroš or John Arne Riise. These players had massive success at Liverpool, in Houllier's treble in 2001 and of course Benítez landed the Champions League in 2005 and FA Cup in 2006. But they could not quite get their hands on the Premier League title.
>
> Cup competitions can be easier to win. You might get a lucky draw, and then of course anybody can

beat anybody over 90 minutes. But you can't do that over 38 games, and I think that's what Liverpool found. They didn't quite have players, be that down to not being able to financially afford them or attract them to the club.

By the time Klopp's first season was over, there was a general sense of a shift in the club and city. A sense of both journey and optimism began to fully take hold. For me and so many others, Liverpool Football Club was catching fire. It felt like a transitional period for the city in a manner that would extend well beyond football and cross paths with a broader picture of the city both politically and economically.

Like many areas across the north, by 2015 Liverpool had suffered from the slashing of local authority budgets; vital services were destroyed by years of demolishing austerity under David Cameron and George Osborne. Rotheram says:

> We're an incredibly resilient community, but those five years had a massive impact on working-class communities across the region, hollowing out services and support systems. People lost their jobs, lost their incomes, and many could no longer access the safety nets they relied on. The government stripped away funding from already left behind areas.
>
> Despite the difficulties in people's personal lives, football has always provided people with an escape. The game was something to look forward to every week, where people could push their problems to the back of their mind for a couple of hours and enjoy watching their team.
>
> After a disappointing few years and uncertainty for Liverpool fans, Klopp's appointment finally gave the red half of the region something to feel excited about. This was a world-class manager known for

playing entertaining football – and he had come out of a self-imposed break to give a hope of resurgence.

His timing couldn't have been better, arriving just a month before another significant transfer in the region. In November 2015, the Liverpool City Region signed a historic devolution deal. That was a massive moment for us, marking the beginning of the transferal of power out of the Westminster bubble and into the hands of local people, giving us the ability to chart our own destiny.

It's safe to say that, on both fronts, we haven't looked back since, although Klopp's success is almost impossible for mere mortals to imitate.

Klopp's early tenure had left many feeling like it was a matter of when and not if for Liverpool. It was a perfect match, and the foundations were now fully in place for success. Most importantly, the city and football club had a purpose; therefore, so did the people.

Chapter 3

Enough is Enough

A NOTABLE addition to the Liverpool skyline has been a redeveloped Anfield stadium. Construction of the stadium's Main Stand was completed in 2016, and the Anfield Road end in early 2024 (after a protracted operation that saw appointed contractors, Buckingham Group, fall into administration on the cusp of the new 2023/24 season).

The Main Stand redevelopment coincided with the appointment of Klopp and fell squarely in line with his ethos of creating an environment so hostile, so insufferable that nobody would want to come and play against his Liverpool team there.

The stand was important on many levels. It represented an arguably savvier yet proactive approach to getting things done. Liverpool were making decisions swiftly and moving on from a 'spade in the ground' promise of a new stadium on Stanley Park, which never arrived under Hicks and Gillett.

Fenway's approach to Liverpool has left fans divided. It's a supporter base that demands consideration on future decisions from those calling the shots. As neighbours Everton have found in recent years, when that consideration isn't present and mismanagement starts to seep in, the wrath is often heavy.

Football fans generally apply a sense of responsibility to their owners for numerous varying interests. Some want the biggest transfer war chest around, while others want to see the bedrock for a secure future amid the uncertain world of Premier League finances. For Liverpool, there's a need to understand tradition and respect 'the Liverpool way', a term that often remains undefined and adaptable, depending on context.

Prior to Hicks and Gillett, Liverpool were in the hands of the late David Moores and his chief executive, Rick Parry. The Moores family held their stake in the club for over 50 years, gaining their wealth through the Littlewoods franchise. The selling of the club to such unfit owners would leave Moores heartbroken. He reportedly felt greatly responsible for the civil war that had broken out inside the club not two years later. Parry famously quipped that 'you only sell the family silver once', but neither could see behind the charm of the Americans at the bidding table, whose credentials, once vetted, were deemed sound enough for club shareholders.

Many assume the impact of representation at ownership level is only felt domestically. What isn't appreciated is how bad feeling towards custodians impacts those supporters from the same country.

Michael MacCambridge is a journalist and editor from Austin, Texas. He talks about the perceptions of Liverpool's American owners since Moores sold the club in 2007:

> To really understand what FSG meant to me and a lot of American fans, you have to go back to the attitude that English football fans have towards US supporters, which is that we're unsophisticated and unknowledgeable.
>
> So those of us who have come to love football were sensitive about that because we wanted to be part of the clan and viewed as real supporters as well. But then you get Hicks and Gillett, who are clearly in over their heads – the 'ugly Americans abroad' – and it was embarrassing. Hicks and Gillett were confirming every stereotype that Liverpool and other English fans had about Americans getting involved with football.

Then there was this inflexion point where New England Sports Group (later Fenway Sports Group) buys the club and I remember wishing that I could write an op-ed in the *Liverpool Echo*, saying: 'Hey, these are different Americans. You may be slow to warm to them, but they're really smart people.'

Although there has been things FSG has done that I've been critical of, I think you have to say among ownership groups in the Premier League they have to be ranked among the two or three best.

In the modern world of football, the reality is that you want to have some hard-hearted capitalists on your side if you want to succeed. Unless you want to be Leeds United and lapse into irrelevance, you want smart numbers people who can make efficient business decisions if you're not going to be owned by a Middle Eastern petrostate – which I don't think most Liverpool fans want.

Both ownerships underestimated Liverpool's cultural and social impact; the difference was that John W. Henry and FSG were smart enough to adjust and change their approach. Instead of sending out insulting emails from spoilt sons of owners [as Tom Hicks Jnr did in 2007], FSG recalibrated and reinvested.

I understand that if you were brought up in Liverpool and stood on the Kop every other Saturday, you would rather have the team owned by a leftist, responsible, socialist billionaire from the city. If you can tell me who that is, I would get on board, but I don't think such a person exists right now.

That's the dose of real-world reality. I think the venture was more complicated than either of those ownership groups could imagine at the beginning, but to the credit of John Henry, Mike Gordon and FSG, they adapted a lot quicker.

When they acquired Liverpool, the line out of Boston was that FSG would be careful and astute stewards of the club, who wouldn't shout from the rooftops about achievements not yet reached – a quite overt barb in the direction of their predecessors, perhaps. To that end, they've been justified in this pledge.

FSG are in every sense underwhelming and at times incredibly aloof. They read the Liverpool people perfectly in this sense. A local disdain towards ostentatious behaviour stems from the expectation to share some of what you have to help others, and not to put on airs in the face of surrounding struggle.

There are also the putrid stereotypes created by the likes of Harry Enfield in the 1980s and 1990s, which led to fans being confronted with poverty chanting. These have reemerged in recent years, noticeably coinciding with Klopp and Liverpool's on-pitch success. FSG went about their business in a way that wasn't brash or chauvinistic, despite the need for constant showstopping drama from the franchise they'd entered into.

They also, however, got things horribly wrong. They may have been learning on the job, but some of the mistakes made have been almost calamitously damaging to the image of responsible custodians. Among the lowest was a leading hand in a Super League breakaway in spring 2021, when, along with other major club owners, they decided to launch a coup to move the game away from its conventional set-up and create a league that united teams across Europe. The aim was to have more autocracy over the pre-eminent sporting entertainment product on the planet.

It was felt that Henry and Fenway believed Liverpool were being domineered by governing bodies and television companies. They believed the club lacked control over their image, viewing and distribution rights, and were essentially propping up those around them. Perhaps the gravest consequence of the Super League was UEFA's ability to martyr themselves as paragons of virtue and tradition.

This wasn't FSG's first rash foray. They'd previously acted without consulting their most important stakeholders – subsequently learning the hard way from fans was perhaps the most frustrating outcome of all. In February 2016, just months after Klopp took over as Liverpool manager, supporters walked out of a match against Sunderland at Anfield in the 77th minute in protest of newly planned £77 tickets, which were due to be made available in the Main Stand when it opened in time for the 2016/17 season.

The city's history with protest is a familiar one. Throughout the despised Margaret Thatcher reign as prime minister, Liverpool wore the cloth of rebellion against a government that questioned whether investment in the city would represent 'pumping water uphill', as then Chancellor of the Exchequer Geoffrey Howe put it.

Liverpool is a place that has never been one for taking its lot. It has stood up to the establishment from as early as the 1911 transport workers strike, which led to crowds and police clashing violently at St George's Plateau. The disturbances came after a demonstration by workers in support of a seamen's strike erupted into violence. Both sailors and fire unions had demanded better pay and conditions for their workers and this spread to UK ports, including Liverpool. Although terms were agreed nationally within days, Liverpool continued to strike, leaving many factories shut and around 250,000 workers protesting. Those workers came together on 13 August outside St George's Hall, when around 80,000 people were met by heavy-handed tactics from Liverpool City Police.

Two days of riots followed, spooking national government and leading to Prime Minister Winston Churchill enlisting the army. Brutality followed, leading to the deaths of two men – docker Michael Prendergast and carter John Sutcliffe, both of whom were shot dead. Four days later, Churchill ordered HMS *Antrim* – a British Navy gunboat – to patrol the Mersey, but the strike was already spreading around the UK.

The story of Churchill 'pointing a gunboat at the city', as it's locally told, promotes the power of union, but also bookmarks Liverpool's sense of rebellion through action: through people's voices being heard, however long it takes.

For many who would walk out of Anfield on a winter's day over a century on, the same sense of principle around fairness was followed with conviction in action. The owners' lack of communication helped drive fans to the exits. Nobody at the club had seemingly conversed with fan groups such as Spirit of Shankly; instead the decision was made in a manner that felt dismissive.

For most, it was – as the chant went that day – a case of enough is enough. Liverpool's average household salary ranges from £28,000 to £34,000 annually. This hasn't fluctuated over the years, and therefore a stable and affordable ticket pricing scheme isn't seen as an unreasonable request from those who reside here. The club would argue that the Main Stand pricing bracket was aimed at its more corporate supporter base and would help drive down touting; but there would be no leeway, and fans streamed to the exits early as Liverpool squandered a two-goal lead to eventually draw 2-2.

Klopp wasn't present that day, after being struck down with a bout of appendicitis, but later said of it, 'There is always a reason for a situation like there was on Saturday. It was not a situation where one game you have 40,000, the next 39,000, the next 38,000, 37, 36 and so on.' He would also call it 'my problem too' and claimed it was 'easy to understand' why fans decided to leave the stadium and, ultimately, the team. Some viewed this as a peacekeeping plea, a call to end a ceasefire so that his objective of winning football matches could be met.

In part, this was true. Klopp is a manager who needs everyone together. He always needs to harness unity for his impact to truly be felt. But supporters noticed an authenticity about Klopp; his response offered people a peak into his true values, which gave insight as to why he took the role of Liverpool manager.

Whether this should matter at all is a topic for debate. There are many who will tell you that mixing football with issues of social equality and government policy is something that shouldn't occur under any circumstances. Yet Liverpool fans have long stood up for their own sense of devastating injustice, which stemmed in the main from Hillsborough. They've also fought the corner of others: from ensuring ticket prices for matches across the Premier League remained reasonable for all, to a banner in the away end of Chelsea in 2018 showing support for the Grenfell Tower tragedy.

There was an early sense that Klopp understood these actions. To the many who witnessed first-hand the impact a manager can have, this was more than welcomed. But the antithesis is also a possibility. Roy Hodgson did many things wrong as a football coach during his time at the club, yet it was his horrifically timed quips about Liverpool's status as a city and club that riled most. Hodgson couldn't buy into the fact that fans should be interested in anything other than taking what's given to them on the pitch (which was of no consolation to anyone who had to watch Liverpool under his tenure). Instead, he came out with a set of what felt like microaggressions, which wouldn't be forgiven. When Liverpool were perilously nosediving towards the prospect of administration, and supporters chose to oppose the disastrous ownership of Hicks and Gillett, Hodgson's response to another protest at Anfield was that 'those people [the protestors] aren't making my job any easier'.

Very early, it became apparent that Klopp understood what it took for Liverpool to be united and responsible for its own success. In the ticket protest, he witnessed people standing up for an issue that meant something more than football. It became linked to the values of a place through decades and generations of what's seen to be an acceptable way of going about things.

Klopp has always gravitated to clubs who represent the working-class values he seems to be aligned with. Mainz, his first managerial love, is an independent city and forms part of the Frankfurt Rhine-Main Metropolitan Region. As of 2023, its population stood at 230,003. As of April 2022, the number of unemployed at the labour offices in Mainz was 193,409, of which 88,066 were long-term unemployed, leaving an unemployment rate of 7.2 per cent. Liverpool had an unemployment rate of 4.4 per cent as of September 2023.

Citing promotion with Mainz as his greatest achievement, Klopp knew early on that involvement was key to showing people that a football club was something to get behind. He also understood that it was a complete escape from the challenges of everyday life, yet also representative of the dedication they'd shown by going to work all week and getting there. He knew he couldn't have a situation like the walkout ever again because, ultimately, he knew that meant the club was doing something that acted to divide rather than unite. All of this leaves a complex portrait of a place, which is at times difficult to understand, especially without knowledge and understanding of its history.

MacCambridge echoes this sensation:

> When, as an outsider, you travel to Liverpool, you do so with a measure of respect and deference. I understand that the Merseyside derby is never going to mean to me what it means to somebody who grew up in a culture of Reds and Blues. I understand that I wasn't there during managed decline and Thatcherism and those things. I understand

part of that is going to escape me, but I try to be understanding and respectful.

At the same time, there are some things that I see from 5,000 miles away which might be more difficult to see if you're at Anfield every other week. Sometimes that's a sense of the crowd. Before Klopp, it was clear how heavy the shirt was for players and easy to identify this invisible force as soon as something went wrong at Anfield.

When I started watching Liverpool in the late 1990s, it was so hard to see games in America. You would find an Irish pub which opened at six in the morning and there would be me and six other people, three of whom were drunk expats bellowing that we were rubbish whether we were winning or not. It made me understand the mindset and widespread negativity that existed.

I think there's a responsibility that most Liverpool fans I know take very seriously, which is about understanding the culture, the history and the meaning of the club. And that it's not just: 'Hey, I like this club because I like the kit.'

Chapter 4
This Is Football

BY THE time Liverpool had embarked on the 2017/18 campaign, the green shoots of Klopp's formation and systemic changes were well and truly blossoming. He'd added Mohamed Salah (Roma), Alex Oxlade-Chamberlain (Arsenal), Dominic Solanke (Chelsea) and Andrew Robertson (Hull City) to the impressive debut seasons of Sadio Mané and Gini Wijnaldum. Virgil van Dijk and Naby Keïta would arrive later, following transfer work done that summer. Philippe Coutinho's protracted move to Barcelona for £142m eventually went through in January 2018.

It was the work Klopp was doing on the training pitch that provided the greatest evidence of progression. A 2016 training camp in California's Palo Alto had journalists in awe when given snippets of sessions. Accompanying double, sometimes triple, daily training were the patterns of play whenever a player lost possession: when and where to press the ball. Also noted was the influence of Arrigo Sacchi and Wolfgang Frank in the shape and set-up across Liverpool's defensive line.

A key driver in those sessions was Pepijn Lijnders – the Dutch coach brought in during Rodgers's reign to develop talent in Liverpool's academy and create a pathway to the first team. Klopp had elevated Lijnders's role in his first season, putting him in charge of a 'development group', whereby young players such as Trent Alexander-Arnold would be brought to Melwood for exposure and participation in the first-team environment.

Klopp saw a passion in Lijnders that he loved. The coach was exuberant and knowledgeable, sharing the same ethos of how the game should be played with high-tempo, aggressive football counterbalanced by a clever defensive structure. When he first took charge, Klopp was in contact with Mike Gordon, who had recommended Lijnders as a coach he might like. He later phoned Gordon to pronounce: 'I don't like him ... I love him.'

It was Lijnders's progression that eventually led him to leave Liverpool and take a management role at NEC Nijmegen in the second tier of the Netherlands in January 2018. He would return that summer as Klopp's assistant following the sudden departure of Željko Buvač – the man Klopp had entrusted as 'the brain' during his success at Dortmund.

Buvač's departure had Liverpool fans worried. To many it had hints of when Houllier's highly rated coach, Patrice Bergues, departed and the team was never the same. History would prove that Lijnders would have been a far more devastating loss than either Bergues or Buvač if Nijmegen hadn't sacked him after failing to win promotion.

At the end of 2016/17, Klopp had restored Champions League football to Liverpool – a competition rich in sentimental history with the club. Take a walk into the city centre and you'll be met with stickers on traffic lights from ultras sections of supporters – Bayern Munich, K.R.C. Genk and FC Porto – who have all left their calling card in recent years.

Supporters come to a city proud to show itself off. Liverpool needs European football to feel its true sense of worth as a place of cultural worth. When economic depression was rife in the 1970s and 1980s, exploring Europe's greatest cities gave people from Liverpool a brief form of escapism. It was also where the term 'casual culture' was formed. Known also as football fashion or terrace fashion, it involved seeking out the most stylish yet informal looks on the Continent and embracing brands such as Adidas and Lacoste. Casual culture would go on to dominate the look of the city and paved the way for iconic shops such as Wade Smith to open.

It still exists. Recent excursions following the Reds abroad have heralded the sight of young Liverpool supporters sporting baseball caps adorned with the logo of opposition teams. This was their badge of honour, a sign they'd been around some of the most recognised and obscure places possible supporting their team and had something to show for it.

Liverpool adopts a sense of symbiosis with fashion. Harsh winters and a piercing wind from the Mersey ensure mountain wear is never out of place, with brands such as The North Face, Monterrain and Under Armour doing a better trade than in most other cities. It's easy to differentiate from the affiliations to Stone Island and Burberry, which influence parts of football culture from the south of England. There are certain labels that bring with them undeniable stereotypes associated to hooliganism and 'firm' culture.

Liverpool has a new generation carrying on traditional values less associated with organised violence. The Spion Kop group, who organise the decorative flags and banners on the Kop in Anfield, is mostly made up of young supporters who yearned for their own sense of purpose and identity in a historically successful club.

Klopp tapped into the fans' perspective that Champions League football was pivotal, recognising the scale of the club early. After they'd secured European football for the 2017/18 season, he stated that qualification for the competition should be 'the minimum requirement' every season.

There was a feeling among many that Liverpool could do something special in Europe the following season. There was a sense among supporters that, if the draw was kind enough, Liverpool would hand out some serious punishment to teams that underestimated the devastation of the new attacking line-up Klopp had built.

As early on as the qualifying round against Hoffenheim, it was clear this was going to be the case. Liverpool had won 2-1 in Germany and returned to Anfield to put on a blistering display of attacking, if somewhat erratic, football. When Emre Can put the hosts 3-0 up within 22 minutes after a sumptuous back-to-front move, Klopp turned to the Main Stand with a raised clenched fist and let out a defiant scream of 'this is football'. At that point, everyone knew Liverpool would be going on a European adventure that so many would fall in love with.

Liverpool played half the season with four attackers – Coutinho, Firmino, Mané and Salah. The Egyptian was lighting up the Premier League in his second stint. Klopp used Salah from the right to devastating effect; in doing so, he shifted Mané left and the pair became a synergy of unpredictability, work rate and world-class talent, which only further evolved after Coutinho's departure.

The development of Robertson from December onwards exemplified Liverpool's increasing competence in assessing potential value through underlying statistics. This was due in no small part to the astute workings of Gordon, Sporting Director Michael Edwards, and chief scouts Barry Hunter and Dave Fallows.

The season ebbed and flowed for Liverpool. Domestically, Manchester City under Pep Guardiola were proving a tour de force, eventually going on to finish with a record 100 points. They would remain unbeaten until a visit to Anfield in January 2018. Klopp's Liverpool produced a 4-3 win, which set a precedent for Guardiola's team's susceptibility to the sheer power of Anfield's atmosphere. The home team swarmed all over the visitors to send Liverpool into a blitzing 4-0 lead at one point. Guardiola was left shell-shocked and helpless on the sidelines.

The match was remembered most for Robertson's lung-busting chase of City players, which went all the way back to their goalkeeper and eventually out of play. The whole stadium erupted as the Scot chased the ball like a dog in a park. He displayed a hunger akin to a player in relegation dogfight, which is exactly what he had been the previous season.

A Klopp strength has been to nurture such battling qualities and develop players physically and technically. Robertson, Gini Wijnaldum, Salah and Mané are only a few examples of the manager's consistency in this area since his days with Mainz.

The victory against City was repeated in the Champions League quarter-final three months later, when Liverpool raced into an early lead and won the first leg 3-0. It was enough to send them to their first semi-final since 2008.

Klopp knew the influence of the crowd was giving new life to a historic stadium. There was now solid evidence that when the place became angry and got behind the team, they could beat anyone on any form. City knew it, too. Guardiola would later go on to say in an interview with a Spanish broadcaster: 'The motto "This Is Anfield" is no marketing spin. There is something about it that you will find in no other stadium in the world. They score a goal and for the next five minutes you feel like you'll receive another four. You feel small and rival players seem to be all over [you].'

Liverpool were exasperating on the pitch. They could score and concede with relative ease in a manner that left matches feeling like tennis rallies. Klopp wanted more control but had to embrace where he and the club were. Crucially, his supporters were along for the journey.

After a 2-1 defeat at Old Trafford to Manchester United on 10 March 2018, that unity grew stronger. Any defeat at United is gut-wrenching for Liverpool supporters across the globe, but this one was met with a sense of pure defiance through song. After the away supporters were routinely held back inside the stadium at full time to disperse home fans and potential trouble, a joyous rendition of their latest chant – 'Allez Allez Allez' – bellowed out through the Manchester air.

Back home in Liverpool, local music promotors BOSS Night had screened the match in Liverpool's District venue, a tight and atmospheric event hall in the heart of the Baltic Triangle. After the match, the BOSS music session started. Its headliner,

Jamie Webster, had already learned to adapt his guitar chords to a version of the latest chant. He launched into a rendition that lasted over 15 minutes and was shared and reshared millions of times around the world.

'It was a turning point, especially for BOSS,' says Shaun O'Donnell, a founder of the concept:

> The video [of Webster singing 'Allez Allez Allez'] went around the world in 24 hours and boosted our following by hundreds of thousands. But it was a turning point for the fanbase. There's never been a defeat at Old Trafford which has left us feeling at one and together like that did. We knew we were at the start of a journey.
>
> The atmosphere [in District] after that game was something I've never felt since. It was defiant, electric, it was something special. Yes, we'd been beaten, yes, we were disappointed but when Jamie played 'Allez Allez Allez', it got bigger and bigger, every chorus got louder and louder. It spilled into the street.

BOSS Night is an evolution of *BOSS Magazine* – a Liverpool fanzine that aimed to cover the more cultural aspects of watching Liverpool. It was on a coach back from a fixture with Chelsea in 2011 when O'Donnell – fresh from a summer working on events in Ibiza – was approached by Daniel Nicholson, the magazine founder, about taking it to the next level in the form of a launch party.

The event took place in Static Gallery at the bottom of Renshaw Street and was headlined by the Tea Street Band. All 350 tickets were sold. O'Donnell points out that this wasn't a football gig, per se. There were no Liverpool songs on stage. At a time when social media hadn't yet fully dominated people's social interactions, the event was seen as a coming together for the matchday community. O'Donnell says:

BOSS Mag was a champion for the local music scene. It would really champion local bands like The Maybes?, The Troubadours, Shack, lots of the old-school Liverpool bands. Part of the match reviews were about going to the game and then later finding yourself at a gig that night. The mag was very important culturally. I don't think there's ever been a match report which mentioned football.

A sold-out gig gave everyone confidence that there was potential longevity in what they were doing. At the start of 2012/13, BOSS sessions were formed on Sundays after Liverpool had played at Anfield following midweek exertion in the Europa League. Again, the music brief was covers and classics only.

That led to BOSS being approached by someone asking whether a young lad could play some songs at the start of a gig. That came to be how Webster got involved, O'Donnell recalls: 'Someone asked us if he could get up and play a few songs at the start of one of our gigs; he was only about 16 or 17 at the time.

'It wasn't fellas singing Liverpool songs on stage, it was just covers, even Jamie did covers. The crowd did that very Scouse thing of turning the lyrics into Liverpool songs and making them about Liverpool players.'

Webster's rise to acclaimed solo artist playing sold-out gigs home and abroad is a source of pride to O'Donnell. 'He's here today because of his talent, make no mistake, but BOSS gave him that platform. If BOSS wasn't around, then maybe he couldn't have got on stage to cut his teeth singing Liverpool songs to being on stage at Glastonbury performing his own stuff,' he ponders.

The 2013/14 season put BOSS Night in full swing. They'd outgrown smaller venues to take up a residency at Sound Food and Drink on Duke Street. Events would be put on after big home fixtures such as Everton or the two Manchester clubs.

After Liverpool beat City that season, over 500 people were at the gig; they poured out on to the street, which led to some minor damage and the police being called. BOSS had a problem. They brought revenue but, in the eyes of some bar owners, they also brought trouble. The concept would eventually be given a new home at District by Jayne Casey, a founding member of Cream and latterly the Baltic Triangle innovation, who spent time in punk bands Big in Japan, Pink Military and Pink Industry during the 1980s.

'She took us in when no one wanted us,' says O'Donnell.

BOSS went from strength to strength as belief in Klopp's Liverpool grew alongside it. In many ways the stars perfectly aligned for both. O'Donnell recognises the grasping of moments being key to the success of both:

> The secret to BOSS's success has been to not overdo it. We could've quite easily done gigs after every game. Our thing has always been to make it a bit more special. It's about creating moments as opposed to it becoming the norm.
>
> To coin a Klopp phrase, 'we've been lucky' – lucky that Klopp has been around at this time, that Jamie was around. I'm extremely proud.

The season would culminate in a Champions League Final against Real Madrid in Kyiv – a place aesthetically beautiful and stoically charismatic, now deep in the devastation of warfare at the hands of Russian invasion. Madrid proved too wily for Klopp's Liverpool on the night. Salah's injury at the hands of Sergio Ramos and a horrendous night for goalkeeper Loris Karius, who was later found to be suffering with concussion, underplayed a 3-1 defeat.

For supporters leaving the stadium there seemed only a mild feeling of a missed opportunity for what could have been. Everyone was under the illusion Liverpool would ensure there was not another decade in the wilderness to follow. There was a growing sense the journey was just beginning, and that Liverpool could go again, and go one better. This would prove to be the case in Madrid, a year on, when Jordan Henderson finally lifted Liverpool's sixth European champions title.

For supporters, the sense of resolve at full time in Ukraine was perhaps emboldened by events earlier that day in Shevchenko Park. A green space in the centre of Kyiv named after Ukrainian writer, poet, artist and political figure, Taras Shevchenko, was turned Liverpool red. The park had been allocated for Liverpool to host fans during the day, with well-known names such as BOSS, *The Anfield Wrap* and Redmen TV all given allotted stage times. The club was working closer than ever with associated groups, which resembled Klopp's one-focus approach.

Walking along the city streets in the park's direction, you could hear sways of chant with every gentle breeze. Billowing red smoke rose from the trees. Fencing had been replaced by flags adorned with the names of Liverpool boroughs, pubs and witty captions. Once inside, Shevchenko Park was like Liverpool's very own Narnia; a stunningly infused landscape of red, green and sunlight yellow. For every break of light there was a plume of pyrotechnics. Most importantly, there was a feeling of euphoria and celebration in a safe space. The Ukrainian police were immaculate, and trusted supporters to behave reasonably, which they of course did.

O'Donnell recalls:

> Kyiv will always be the best time I've had doing BOSS and following Liverpool. What happened [in Shevchenko Park] that day was something nobody at this club has done before. I remember walking from the park to the stadium feeling ten feet tall. It's why I felt nobody was too upset when we lost.

It was in a far-out place and a venue nobody knew anything about. It felt more underground because it was smaller scale. It was the first time we'd taken BOSS on the road, not knowing how it would be working with the club or if anyone would even turn up.

It's horrible to see where [Ukraine] is now after how brilliant they were. If District was the turning point for togetherness, Kyiv was the gathering. This was the company conference where we agreed on our goals going forward as a supporter base. It was impossible to describe the buzz of smiling faces, happy with optimism because of what Klopp had done and was doing.

The emotion could be directed back to Klopp and what he's given us. We were there to follow Liverpool, but it felt like Klopp had given us something back we hadn't had for so long. He's brought togetherness and connection for the first time in my match-going life.

We've had successful times but there's always been that disconnect in the crowd where one fella disagrees with another fella. Some have been behind the manager, and some haven't. I think it's undoubtable that everyone is behind Klopp, and he has everybody singing from the same hymn sheet.

I think what he's done with local organisations such as BOSS, Spion Kop, *The Anfield Wrap*, Spirit of Shankly has been brilliant. They always existed before Klopp, but I don't think the connection to the club was as transparent to what it is now.

What he's brought is the ability to treat every single person like a human being. He's shared beers with people I know through BOSS and made them feel like they're one of the players. I can't think of another manager in the world who could do that.

There is often an accusation of naval-gazing levelled at Liverpool. A perception that people are self-indulgent and believe they're exceptional in aspects of support, protest or cultural awareness. While it's impossible to comment on the experience of others, Liverpool supporters will inevitably draw on those early Klopp years with reverence and fondness. The feeling of anticipation and unique sense of togetherness was impossible to shift. Liverpool had something to believe in, and this time they weren't to be denied.

Part 2

Inclusion

Chapter 5

The Liverpool Model

LIVERPOOL'S RELATIONSHIP with representation and equality is not always an easy discussion. A city that once profited from a booming slave trade, walking around the leafy suburbs of the Georgian Quarter exposes the dark past of the streets and those who gave their names to them.

Consider Rodney Street, which was named after Admiral George Rodney, a key supporter of the slave trade towards the end of the 18th century. Admiral Rodney rose to prominence after leading a victorious battle against France in 1782 in the West Indies. As well as being a vocal supporter of slavery, he traded sugar from plantations in Jamaica using slave labour.

Even the world-renowned Penny Lane has come under intense scrutiny in recent years, after links to notorious slave trader James Penny emerged. It was later established that no credible ties to Penny Lane being named after him could be found, leaving the origins of its roots a general mystery.

Attention was drawn to many of Liverpool's street and road names during the Black Lives Matter protests, which followed the death of George Floyd at the hands of Minneapolis police officers. This led then mayor of Liverpool, Joe Anderson, to admit that the council 'hasn't done anywhere near the amount or the things it should have done to help minority groups'. This was later followed up with the formation of a Race Equality Task Force, which was set up by the local authority to tackle race-related inequality in the city. The official website doesn't hold back on the stark figures, describing how 'police in Merseyside are twice as likely to stop and search Black people, unemployment is 8.4% higher for people from Black and Minority Ethnic backgrounds in the city than it is for others, and Covid-19 has brought these inequalities into sharp relief'.

Football on Merseyside has always refracted the politics of its time. When John Barnes backheeled a banana skin off the pitch at Goodison Park in 1988, it became an iconic image despite how his reaction sat against such depressingly routine racist behaviour. The perception seemed that football was riddled with racism, hooliganism and a lack of education within society. Such behaviours seemed to be tolerated or, worse, appeared to be accepted.

Liverpool themselves were mired in unwanted controversy after Luis Suárez was found guilty of racially abusing Manchester United defender Patrice Evra following a confrontation during the Premier League encounter at Anfield on 16 November 2011. Suárez was alleged to have used 'insulting words', which included a reference to Evra's colour. A Liverpool statement at the time now makes for difficult reading:

> We find it extraordinary that Luis can be found guilty on the word of Patrice Evra alone. No one else on the field of play – including Evra's own Manchester United teammates and all the match officials – heard the alleged conversation between the two players in a crowded Kop goalmouth.
>
> It appears to us that the FA were determined to bring charges against Luis Suárez, even before interviewing him at the beginning of November. Nothing we have heard in the course of the hearing has changed our view that Luis Suárez is innocent of the charges brought against him and we will provide Luis with whatever support he now needs to clear his name.

The incident was certainly one the entire club learned from. Manager Kenny Dalglish and the players stood firmly and publicly behind Suárez without fully considering the impact of their actions or its wider message. Football has tried to make strides to improve on discrimination, but not enough has been done. Instead, incidents from the past return and reoccur: as with Barnes in the 1988 Merseyside derby, 30 years later a banana skin was thrown at Pierre-Emerick Aubameyang in a 2018 North London derby. Sadly, the present is never too far from the past.

What is clear during Klopp's time at Liverpool, and long before that, is that football clubs and their impact matter on every level of society. Liverpool currently have two non-white players from the city in their first-team squad: vice-captain Trent Alexander-Arnold and Toxteth-raised Curtis Jones.

'Our kids can see a pathway from Trent and Curtis. They're examples of people who walk, talk and dress like us,' says Earl Jenkins, the chair and coach of Kingsley United, a community football club with 12 teams of varying age, gender and background. Kingsley are based on the recently refurbished Tiber pitches on the back of Lodge Lane in Liverpool 8. For Earl, the wider importance and messaging football offers has never been lost on the local community:

> They've never had that [inspiration] before and it gives them the early incentive to push and sacrifice if that's what they want.
>
> But we know football is a short career. And we also know you're more likely to be a bank manager than Premier League footballer. That's why we emphasise the need for a Plan B. The two teams make every kid growing up want to be a footballer. They see Trent at Liverpool and it gives them hope they can have that one day.

> We'd love to create professional footballers, but our priority is to create good people for the community so that they're not involved in crime and having a negative impact. We teach young people how to be good citizens who have support through education. We use football to help with every part of a young person's life.

Around Anfield, walls are now adorned in tribute to current and past idols. Alexander-Arnold, Firmino and Salah have their own section of decorated brick and mortar in L4. Given that mural art often represents social championing and a celebration of values, the presence of Black and Muslim players held in shrine-like reverence does truly represent progress.

In the wake of Floyd's murder, the entire Liverpool squad was pictured around the circle of the pitch, perched down on one knee. A symbol of passive resistance to establishment brutality, which was seen as the prime cause of Floyd's asphyxiation. The symbol remains in circulation within the game to this day and is routinely applauded around most stadiums prior to kick-off, including at Anfield. While no longer a weekly occurrence, for the 2023/24 season players pledged to take the knee at the Premier League's opening and final match rounds of the season, as well as dedicated 'No Room for Racism' fixtures in October and April, and on Boxing Day. Klopp said:

> For us, dealing with each other and Black Lives Matter is very natural – especially if you look at our team: we have players from Africa, from England and so on with a corresponding background.
>
> It is already so natural for us that at first we didn't even think about sending a message. But then the boys were struck. Then they spontaneously decided on this action. I've been very proud of the guys for a long time, but that was another extraordinary

moment. When I saw them there and this picture was taken. Then I was really proud because it is also an important message.

In every geographical and iconic sense, the area of Toxteth and Liverpool's L8 district embodies so much of its city's identity. It holds within it all of Liverpool's texture and tension around equality. It is, of course, mostly synonymous with the nine days of rioting in 1981, during which Merseyside Police stated that 468 police officers were injured, 500 people were arrested and at least 70 buildings were damaged so severely by fire that they had to be demolished. Around 100 cars were damaged or destroyed and there was extensive looting of shops.

The riots were a call to action. They represented the overspill of racial prejudice at the hands of law enforcement coupled with Margaret Thatcher's policies linked to her beliefs in monetarism and neoliberalism. These ideologies were nurtured alongside her chief economic advisers, Alan Walters and Patrick Minford – the latter a professor at Liverpool University at the start of the 1980s.

Thatcher's lingering reputation in the city is the persistent refrain of 'managed decline', an approach she was encouraged to take with Liverpool by her chancellor, Geoffrey Howe. In released government files, Howe described economic investment in the city as 'pumping water uphill' and that Thatcher should be wary 'not to overcommit scarce resources to Liverpool'.

How much of this approach Thatcher unofficially embraced remains a moot point. What was apparent was her desire to control the supply of money to curb inflation. She would combine this with low taxation on the very richest, the 'one per cent' as it's often referenced. Her ideals of free-market ideology and trickle-down economics proved disastrous for parts of England already struggling with increased deindustrialisation. Industries that were propping up local communities were disappearing, and those who were already suffering from deprivation were being plunged further into poverty.

Toxteth was just one of those areas ravaged by decline, stagnation and central government neglect. An area heavily bombed in the Second World War, Toxteth was encumbered by fly-tipped waste ground and derelict houses, stretching towards Liverpool's docks, which were within half a mile of Toxteth's Upper Parliament Street. It needed desperate help, but instead it became a government case study called 'The Liverpool Model'. The initial versions of the model assumed, like many Thatcherites, that the country's 'natural' rate of unemployment was low. They thought that purging the economy and causing further urban decay would mean, at worst, hundreds of thousands of redundancies, rather than millions.

'In the Liverpool Model, we were too optimistic about the speed with which the economy would ... come right,' Minford admitted to *The Guardian* in 2015. 'Although we were closer than many of the pessimists. The bit we were way out on was unemployment.'

Unemployment, heavy-handed policing and the draining of local authority and benefit funding ultimately pushed Toxteth over the edge. A battle ensued and Tory minister Michael Heseltine – an outspoken critic of Thatcher – was seconded from Westminster to Liverpool.

Heseltine is a fascinating character. He was viewed as a pariah within Thatcher's government (one of the more vocal 'wets'), and the decision to send him to Liverpool at the height of its struggle was seen as throwing him to the wolves. But Heseltine noticed both value and potential in Liverpool. He would play a role in revolutionising its celebrated waterfront from abandoned wasteland to today's Albert Dock, a highly popular tourist destination. After being inspired by post-war Germany, his arrangement in 1984 for a garden festival to be created within the derelict site was an example of him contributing to its rebirth, but doing so in an imaginative, even daring way.

He also spoke with consideration to Black communities when pressed on causation factors related to unrest in Toxteth and Brixton, stating: 'We talk of equality of opportunity. What do those words actually mean in the inner cities today? What do they mean to the Black communities? We now have large immigrant communities in British cities. Let this party's position be absolutely clear: They are British. They live here. They vote here.'

The history and evolution of Toxteth is unique, yet it remains a community that acts as a microcosmic exemplifier of what makes the city shine brightest. That includes the influence of its football teams. Like everywhere else with an L postcode, the community will always be divided Red or Blue. It will always be influenced by heritage. It will wear all its trauma openly as part of its beauty.

This goes far beyond preference or tribalism. Football can be a protective channel from the temptations of crime and the societal issues that some youngsters have to face. They need worthy role models and ones who represent them both physically and emotionally. Liverpool's football clubs will always be adored unconditionally; they're imbued with eternal idolisation from one generation to another.

But there have been particular markers in Klopp's approach to football, and to life, which have helped to knit different communities together. From Kingsley United to the local community, Jenkins agrees that Klopp's attitude has rallied areas within Merseyside's growing population of diverse culture and ethnicity:

> His character and personality shine. He listens to what fans are saying and when he talks our youngsters listen. It's great that his team are doing lots more in the community and that has to come from the manager in some form.

We attribute a lot of what happens on and off the pitch to Klopp. You have to feel this city. You have to be entrenched by it and I think he'll be regarded as one of the greats because he has done that. He's someone who seems to find a relatability here he can harness. Even the fist-pumps at the end of the game are a lesson in togetherness and emotion. People at all ages thrive off that in this city. When we feel that sense of a genuine character, we'll back you.

Toxteth is now one of Liverpool's most exciting and positively energised communities. It's a place that inspires and is inspired in equal measure. Klopp has offered the area something to grasp with his messaging of inclusion. For this particular place, it could hold no greater sway.

Chapter 6

If You're Alone, You're Weaker than the Unit

THE NUMBER 58 has no real relevance to Liverpool. The number stands out in football as being the year of the Munich air disaster – the tragedy that saw 23 people, including eight Manchester United players and three officials, fatally injured when a plane tried to take off from a runway in Munich-Riem airport on 6 February 1958.

Locally on Merseyside, only the number 58 bus – which runs from the Litherland area through Jamie Carragher's old haunt of Marsh Lane, Bootle and on into the city centre – offers any plausible link to the number.

In 2016, when England held a referendum on whether it should leave the European Union, 58.2 per cent of Liverpool's registered population voted in favour of remaining. Overall, the country voted to leave by a threadbare majority, something that Klopp became vocal on in its reverberating aftermath. In 2018, he told *The Guardian*:

> When Mr [David] Cameron had the idea [of a referendum] you thought: 'This is not something people should decide in a moment.' We are all influenced by the way only some of the argument is given, and once the decision is taken nobody gives you a real opportunity to change it again. The choice was either you stay in Europe, which is not perfect,

or you go out into something nobody has any idea how it will work.

The EU is not perfect, but it was the best idea we had. History has always shown that when we stay together, we can sort out problems. When we split then we start fighting. There was not one time in history where division creates success. So, for me, Brexit still makes no sense.

It has been viewed as surprising that Klopp gives his opinion on matters such as this. To some extent it's seen by certain Liverpool fans as unhelpful or divisive. By his own standards, he answers such questions in the way he knows best: honestly. His ability to distil and simplify complicated issues makes him the ideal respondent to such probes. He can be spiky (at times, confrontational) on matters of football, but most of the time it's him bringing clarity in a way that makes sense. When doing so to football supporters, who generally want to see things in a similar way, he has a way of cutting through the complexities.

This is very much Klopp's style. He speaks in a manner familiar with many Germans who bear the weight of their own history; he can tell of cautionary tales because he has lived in their shadow since birth. If Germans can generally carry their history with the appropriate level of decorum and self-awareness, those bearing the Union Jack and St George flag are often viewed in wider football and political circles as nationalist to the point of pomposity. Chants about winning wars have become synonymous with England's national football team support, as well as other unsavoury elements.

It's difficult to view Klopp as a bridge in this sense, given how tribal football is. He has been sensible on most issues faced, but the perpetual hunt for the 'narrative' in football is never far away. When Klopp has spoken on the pitfalls of TV scheduling, or the need for five substitutes as opposed to three, he has sometimes been criticised (rather than the far more logical conclusion that he raises these points for the benefit of everyone in the game).

His knack for sensibility and pragmatism has been acknowledged in different forms. In 2021 he became the first winner of the German-British Freundship Award, which was set up to honour the relationship between the two nations. In April 2022 Klopp was the subject of a quite astonishing open-letter plea in the *New European*, written by journalist and former spokesperson to Tony Blair, Alastair Campbell. His longing to see Klopp in politics was based on the perception of sound principles and creating togetherness within a group of people. Campbell signed off his letter by saying, 'Thank you for everything you give to our country.'

Klopp's relatability to the people of Liverpool comes from his socialist leanings. The son of a salesman in the modest Glatten region of Germany's Black Forest, Klopp surpassed the modest talent he possessed as a professional player when he began coaching. He later described himself as having 'fourth division talent and a first division brain'. His playing days at Mainz honed the notion of making the people around you happy: Klopp's football is about working hard to entertain fans, especially those who might be working six days a week. There's an inherent belief that every Klopp team needs to show they're willing to give everything they have for 90 minutes on the pitch.

Aside from what Liverpool supporters witness on the pitch, the need to share common values off it remains so imperative that many outside the club find it enraging. Liverpool is a city that has remained a Labour stronghold since Thatcherism took hold after 1979. Its promotion of workers' rights and working-class values lay the basis of ground rules for general conduct in the city. On the Kop, there are flags and chants that oppose Conservative traits (putting it mildly).

Chants of 'fuck the Tories' raining down from the Anfield stands are often instigated as a response to some groups of opposition fans. Their continued penchant for linking

Liverpool to deprivation takes the form of poverty chanting as a particularly low, point-scoring vehicle. The need for a manager to represent the people is perhaps a sign of Liverpool's bunker mentality. It can feel *us against the world*, so the need to have everyone on side is paramount.

'I believe in the welfare state,' Klopp has said. 'I'm not privately insured. I would never vote for a party because they promised to lower the top tax rate. My political understanding is this: if I am doing well, I want others to do well too. If there's something I will never do in my life, it is vote for the right.'

Klopp's roots are firmly planted in Germany's Swabia region in the south-west of the country. It's a region renowned for cultural frugality from its people, along with a penchant for pietism (a 19th-century movement within Lutheranism that emphasised hard work and shunned worldly amusements). It's a culture that doesn't entertain flamboyance or the flaunting of wealth. The people are renowned for making sensible purchases within their means and that are built to last.

All of which is built on hard work. Those type of cultural values can go some way to explaining Klopp's general modesty and understanding of what the people need from a social outlet, and, indeed, whether they get value for money when going to watch his team. Klopp's beliefs lean almost identically into those propagated by Anfield's immortal son Bill Shankly, who was viewed as the ultimate man of the people.

Shankly's legacy remained the benchmark of greatness and representation far beyond his managerial tenure and indeed his life. He was unique to Liverpool in his assertiveness towards the idea that society seeped into football. His pronouncements were often in reference to a 'collective effort', as he called it:

> The socialism I believe in isn't really politics. It is a way of living. It is humanity. I believe the only way to live and to be truly successful is by collective effort,

with everyone working for each other, everyone helping each other, and everyone having a share of the rewards at the end of the day. That might be asking a lot, but it's the way I see football and the way I see life.

Shankly's granddaughter, Karen Gill, believes that the make-up of Liverpool itself definitely impacts its relationship with its football clubs and managers:

> Liverpool has strong working-class roots going back to the beginning of its history and development as a port. Places where the community needs to pull together to protect the vulnerable, weak and sick are generally going to be more socialist in their core values than the other end of the political spectrum and its emphasis on the individual.
>
> The mining village where my granddad grew up inculcated the tenets of socialism into him. Pulling together, working for each other and helping your neighbour were key to his upbringing. I think the people of Liverpool relate to these values. Then there's the rebellious nature of Liverpudlians, which has been strengthened by clashes with the establishment. Socialism is, in my opinion, a fairer more compassionate philosophy, which reflects the ethos of the people of Liverpool.

Within both managers' ideology is the notion that football mirrors society, and the governance they would like to see within it. Looking out for each other and encouraging collaborative thinking are foundational themes that both Shankly and Klopp's Liverpool teams share. They both believed that the harder they worked together for each other, the more collective good would come out of it.

Beyond the yearning for Klopp to head into politics – and return competence to the anarchy that currently exists within British government – the general understanding is that his values are perfect for his current job and he's in exactly the right workplace environment.

Liverpool remains as far away from having a Tory constituency as it has ever been. As pointed out in an article by David Jeffery in *Springer Magazine* from 2017, the Conservative Party was the dominant political force in Liverpool from the mid-18th century and remained so until the middle of the 20th century. Equally, in *Re-Thinking Popular Conservatism in Liverpool: Democracy and Reform in the Later Nineteenth Century*, Sandra O'Leary notes: 'By 1914, the Labour Party occupied only seven of a possible 140 seats on the city council, and it was only in 1955 that Labour achieved its first municipal majority in the city.'

Despite Labour's victory in the mid-1950s, the Conservatives averaged 49.8 per cent of votes cast in local elections in Liverpool in that decade and 51.1 per cent in the 1960s. However, this domination wouldn't survive in the 1970s. In 1972 the Conservatives lost control of the council for the final time and in 1987 failed to return a single councillor.

But Jeffrey argues that the decline in Conservative rule was down to a mid-century rise in Irish religious influence, popularity for the Liberal Party (and its brand of 'pavement politics', which would offer a suitable alternative to the Tory vote), and the emergence of what's described as socialisation. This is the process whereby an individual's beliefs, outlooks and other related values are shaped by the environment in which they find themselves. There's considerable evidence to suggest that the most important period of socialisation – where an individual is most receptive to environmental cues – is during their formative years, between 15 and 25.

It stands to reason, then, that the rise in disdain for Thatcherism and her era as prime minister would shape the voting and political persuasion of a whole new generation of Scousers, whose parents came of age during her leadership. If anything, the sense of anti-Conservative sentiment has only risen in recent years. In Liverpool, even the suggestion of being considered a Tory voter can mark someone out for treason.

That said, to understand why right-leaning politics is so disliked in the city offers little in the way of clarifying what Liverpool is actually striving for politically. It has become shrouded in buffoonery at local council level under Labour rule in recent years; local mismanagement has certainly cloaked the streets in a sense of confusion. The sense of direction isn't very clear. But if football were a barometer, the favouritism towards socialist views among the general match-going atmosphere at Anfield suggests that's what the city would like to see more of, not less.

One of the more overt examples of support to a leftist movement was when then Labour leader Jeremy Corbyn was pictured outside Anfield with supporters from the Spion Kop 1906 group. A banner was later unveiled on the Kop with pictures of Corbyn and his deputy John McDonnell, who originates from Bootle, with the words: 'What unites us is greater than what divides us.' It's notable how many young people are in this picture. How they lead the chants against poverty or Scouse stereotypes when watching Liverpool home and away, and how they crave their own champion.

Klopp's soundbites may seem modest to himself, but for a city that's saturated with hero worship, and values doing the right thing, he ticks more than one vital box. The job description for 'Manager of Liverpool FC' inevitably ends up stretching way beyond coaching footballers and winning matches.

Chapter 7

If it's Good Enough for You, it's Good Enough for Me

THERE'S A common theme residing in Klopp's ethos, which becomes obvious when he introduces a new face into the group of people he nurtures at Liverpool. It's known in some circles to be the 'no dickhead' policy: you get the general point; the manager wants to work with people he likes and trusts. James Milner described the dressing room at Liverpool as not having a single 'wrong-un'.

Klopp needs to understand people as much as he understands players. He delves into their lives, their likes and their motivations in a manner that feels more authentic than that of a voyeuristic manager purveying the lifestyle of a multimillion-pound asset on a tactics board. He was once so dumbfounded that a member of staff didn't know that his latest signing Andy Robertson had recently become a father that he had to walk away from the conversation.

To that end, it's no surprise that two of Liverpool's most recently celebrated forwards, and two bastions of Klopp's revival, have been a source of pride to Liverpool's Islamic community during their time on Merseyside. Both Mohamed Salah and Sadio Mané have been figureheads in driving through cultural barriers in their own ways.

Mané's departure from Liverpool in June 2022 was particularly poignant and sad to see. One of Klopp's first signings, the Senegal forward was an embodiment of the skill

IF IT'S GOOD ENOUGH FOR YOU, IT'S GOOD ENOUGH FOR ME

and work rate Klopp promised his team would deliver. But Mané somehow went over and above. After a win against Leicester City in September 2018, he was filmed the next day cleaning the toilets of a local mosque in Liverpool where he attended to pray. So genuine were his intentions that he'd apparently pleaded for the footage not to be put online.

Another picture had emerged around a year earlier of Mané wearing a thobe and holding the wide-eyed baby of a local fan in an Asda store in Liverpool. He later described the baby as 'surprised'.

Salah, too, has never shied away from his awareness as a local and global icon and role model; it's something he balances with incredible grace. Often stopping and posing for photos with fans, in one notable encounter a youngster, who was so focused on chasing down his car to meet Salah outside Anfield that he careered into a lamppost and was left bloodied and bruised, still managed to get a joyful photograph with his idol.

Salah and Mané both bore the weight of their star status at Liverpool, in addition to the hopes and dreams of their respective countries. They're the among the most recognisable athletes in Africa and carry with them the footballing expectations of their nations. But closer to their adopted home, they've been massively impactful on Liverpool. Every celebration was followed by the practice of the sujud, where they place their head to the ground in a gesture of humbleness to Allah.

The Muslim prayer can also be seen around Anfield Stadium off the pitch. In 2016 a multi-faith prayer room was set up inside the stadium to help fans who needed to pray at certain times throughout the day.

Liverpool fan, Rahat Chowdhury, attended Anfield during the 4-0 win over Manchester United in April 2022. He later tweeted about his experience at the match at a time during Ramadan: 'I was fasting when I went to Anfield yesterday and after I broke my fast I needed a place to pray. I went to the stewards to ask for a place to pray and not only did they escort me to the prayer room outside the ground but they also guided me there, waited for me to finish so I was allowed back in.' Later, he told the *Liverpool Echo*: 'I've genuinely never met such helpful and respectful stewards like this and I feel they should be appreciated especially when they respect something so important as religion to someone like me.'

For Chowdhury, having attended matches this season at other grounds, the experience at Liverpool was by far the best. 'I've been to Arsenal, West Ham, and Luton Town games and even Wembley,' he said. 'No one is accommodating like Liverpool are. It 100% increases my love for the club. It's a very community-based club and they actually care about the fans. The fact they did what they did made it even more special.'

This experience is a welcome change from pictures that emerged during a match at Anfield in 2014. Two Muslim supporters were praying in the concourse of the stadium, and they were photographed by someone who later tweeted the picture alongside the hashtag 'DISGRACE', which was rightly widely condemned.

How much of this positive change has been influenced directly by Klopp remains undefinable. But there's no doubt that a more diverse squad and an accommodating set-up that welcomes awareness of other beliefs and traditions helps with the inclusivity he yearns for at Liverpool.

The discussion around inclusivity stretches far beyond the confines of Anfield's hallowed turf. A population study of Liverpool in 2022 showed that 91 per cent of Liverpool's 911,546 population was defined as White British, Irish or other. That Liverpool remains under-represented in this sense is at odds with its history. The earliest recorded mosque in Britain was founded in a Liverpool terrace house in 1889 when a group of 20 British converts to Islam, led by Sheikh Abdullah William Henry Quilliam, formed the Muslim Institute. A local solicitor raised in a Methodist family, Quilliam had converted to Islam during his travels in Morocco.

Before the founding of the mosque at 8 Brougham Terrace in the city's L8 district, meetings had been held in a small, rented room in nearby Mount Vernon Street. The social and religious mores of Victorian Britain, cleaved to by local residents, resulted in hostility towards this small group of predominately British converts to Islam. They were pelted with eggs and stones and eventually forced to leave the premises due to the landlady's vehement objections.

After Quilliam purchased the house in Brougham Terrace, Liverpool's Muslim community finally enjoyed a stable home. Although the Muslim Institute was adversely affected by continued unrest and demonstrations by local residents, it remained at 8 Brougham Terrace until Quilliam left Liverpool in 1908. After that the building was used as council offices and then fell into disrepair. Recently it has been refurbished by the Abdullah Quilliam Society and reopened as a mosque.

Nuh Hakim-Okomi is a community football coach who works to support disadvantaged young people from Liverpool. He has Nigerian, Somali and Malaysian heritage and is a practicing Muslim. When I asked Nuh to contribute to this book, he described the project as 'exciting' and was supportive of the idea behind it. Through football and influential figures such as Salah and Mané, Nuh believes that hardened perceptions and racial prejudice in the city have softened:

> Before this recent era of success [for Liverpool] there was no need to understand difference. You might see a person on TV or in the city centre but nothing felt close to home. Over the past decade or so the city has changed. Toxteth was the hub of diversity, and that hub has now expanded across the city.
>
> The club has influence. Take Mané as an example; his success and talent has made people shift towards

something different. The profile of Mané leaves individuals open to education through embracing those players' talents and being exposed to different cultures. The madness of Salah and Mané fasting during a Champions League Final provokes curiosity. Children will ask me questions about this. They will ask other Muslims about this whereas before they mightn't.

We've been blessed to have Salah and Mané because they're such big pillars in their communities from Egypt and Senegal. They've done so much to give back to their own cultures and that resonates.

Perhaps this is seen most through an affectionate chant about Salah to the tune of 1996 hit 'Good Enough' by Dodgy, which coined the alternative lyrics 'sitting in a Mosque, that's where I want to be', and 'if he scores another two, then I'll be Muslim too'. The chant remains sung by predominantly non-Muslim Liverpool supporters, who may have previously seen the Muslim faith as something to feel threatened by or scared of.

The sense of education and understanding needs to be a two-way street. For players such as Mané and Salah to carry out their prayers and practices, they need to feel safe and protected by their environment. Liverpool set up specific alterations to their preparations to assist Islamist players with Ramadan: the 29-to-30-day period of fasting between sunrise and sunset that runs from March or April.

Muslims fast during Ramadan in commemoration of the Islamic holy text, the Quran. It's seen as a cleansing of soul and mind, a period of devout restraint from behaviour deemed as sinful, such as swearing and violent thoughts. With around 1.6 billion people taking part annually, understanding Ramadan and other Muslim practices is incredibly important for wider society. Awareness and respect for Ramadan's requirements have improved across football in recent years. The Premier League has opened up dialogue about fixture flexibility as a result of fasting, as well as introducing academies for further information. As part of its 'commitment to championing equality, diversity and inclusion', understanding the observance of Ramadan is also an opportunity to appreciate the implications of a player's performance and preparations.

The world of football is more adaptable today than ever before. Elite conditioning, nutrition and better medical advice means that bodies can be constantly monitored for balance and peak output. There's also a fasting exemption for athletes in certain circumstances, including performance days. Regardless of this, clubs have created bespoke plans to ensure that player performance isn't majorly affected. This ranges from the type of foods consumed to optimising the last intake before sunrise, usually thought to be around 4.30am. It's clear that Liverpool have developed not just a superficial awareness and responsibility to supporters and players from multiple backgrounds, but a genuine attempt to be respectfully inclusive.

Okomi says:

> When I first started going to the game, there was no halal food options, and now most of the meat served is halal, which is massive. Those subtle changes to make things accessible is so important because a sense of belonging is everything. On my second visit to Anfield I was racially abused, and now I don't feel like that would happen because I feel the face of the club has changed. The club have done the really small things well in terms of even celebrating other cultures over the years.

Klopp, for his part, has been vocal about the importance of Ramadan being carried out by his players:

> I have no problem with my players fasting. I respect their religion and they were always amazing whether they were fasting or not. There are days when Mané and Salah come late to the dressing room because they were praying. There are many things more important than football.
>
> I love that we have so much 'multi-culti', I would say [having] the best ambassadors for being a Muslim in the team is really great. Muslims wash their body very often in specific situations. Before warming up, after warming up, it takes time. So we decided to do things differently.

Klopp's unsurprisingly accepting and welcoming views again go a long way to informing the general conversation around fasting with footballers and athletes. The positive impact of an era where many of Liverpool's recent crop of legends are Muslim transcends mere light-hearted chants that hint at a cultural embrace of Islam.

In 2019 a survey carried out by Stanford University found that an 18.9 per cent reduction in hate crime could be attributed to Salah's arrival on Merseyside.

The report, titled 'Can Exposure to Celebrities Reduce Prejudice? The Effect of Mohamed Salah on Islamophobic Behaviours and Attitudes', supports the view that Salah's impact on Merseyside had a wider and more profound impact than just sporting adulation:

> Overall, we interpret these results to support the hypothesis that Salah's arrival at Liverpool FC caused a decrease in extreme acts of bigotry. Research from four university professors is based on 936 county-month hate crime observations, 15 million tweets from British football fans, and an original survey experiment of 8,060 Liverpool fans.

> We find that Merseyside county (home to Liverpool F.C.) experienced an 18.9 per cent drop in hate crimes relative to a synthetic control, while no similar effect was found for other types of crime. We also find that Liverpool F.C. fans halved their rates of posting anti-Muslim tweets (a drop from 7.2 per cent to 3.4 per cent of tweets about Muslims) relative to fans of other top-flight English soccer clubs.

This is by no means a concrete suggestion that issues such as Islamophobia are fixed by football, or that fans will always become model pupils because of the arrival of a non-native player. Locally, Liverpool suffered from a spate of racial and homophobic attacks soon after lockdowns ended in 2021, assaults that came in for widespread condemnation across the city. Yet it's still important to note the influence of the city's football teams as a driver for togetherness and education, considering the evidence of the Stanford study.

Liverpool's success in the recent era definitely correlates with that impact. If Salah, Mané and others represented another underwhelming false dawn for a once omnipotent body, the adulation and hero worship would not be as forthcoming. Klopp would tell you that he brought in footballers who passed his own personality test and that were incredible players to boot. But intentional or not, he opened another door to Liverpool that left its mark on the wider demographic.

According to Okomi:

> We have to accept football as a platform. Sometimes we forget that and take what's happening in elite football personally. Taking the knee was a great example of that. I've seen these discussions around allyship or action, and those actions in football create a conversation to allow for change. What isn't good is when it becomes tokenistic and when people take

the knee because they don't want to be perceived as racist.

Wilfred Zaha has taken a militant approach to taking the knee [by refusing] because he felt that no action was being taken.

But there is still some meaningful allyship in the game, even if the world always needs more. In an effusive piece, journalist Timo Al-Farooq for the *Muslim Vibe* stated how Klopp was the 'white ally' of Muslims and people of colour:

> Klopp goes further than just symbolically defending people of colour and Muslims against white bigotry. He is our ally, fighting the good fight not with organised activism, but with simple individual human decency, one that can be witnessed not only in interviews and press conferences but also in his day-to-day managerial duties of a team that is as ethnically diverse as all the other Premier League clubs. And as Britain itself.

By its mere existence, Liverpool Football Club offers a platform to broaden mindsets. The inclusion of various cultures and religions into a successful team naturally brings with it an organic sense of acceptance. It can be argued that this shouldn't have to be the case, but, fundamentally, what surrounds Klopp's massive success at Liverpool is a sense of integrity, good ethics and a spirit of global community.

To have these positives accentuated in such a way and with such reach is vital – not only in Liverpool, but across the universe.

Chapter 8

'Ello, 'Ello

IT'S A still, August afternoon at Liverpool's AXA training centre in Kirkby. In every sense it's the last place Paul Amann expected to be. That was until a call from the club's fan liaison officer, Tony Barrett, came in the wake of Liverpool's opening-day 4-0 win at Norwich City at the start of the 2021/22 season.

The match itself was routine in that the Reds were known to rack up high-scoring wins at Carrow Road. The 5-4 victory in Klopp's debut season, which led to his glasses being shattered by his jubilant players, remains the ascendant turning point from doubters to believers for most fans. But there was a low point in this highlight. The win was blemished by the adopted Oasis chant on Liverpool's terraces aimed at on-loan Chelsea midfielder Billy Gilmour: 'Hello, hello, Chelsea rent boy, Chelsea rent boy.' The chant has lain dormant without challenge, and, crucially, without understanding for many years. It was vocally aired at those with Chelsea affiliation for years. Objection from those in the LGBTQ+ community has instantly been dismissed through ignorance over its intention not being homophobic. 'Impact matters more than intention,' Amann notes.

In the wake of the match, LGBTQ+ fan group Kop Outs immediately condemned the chanting from the away end at Carrow Road. Kick It Out, football's leading anti-discrimination body, stated: 'We are absolutely clear: the "rent boy" chant is homophobic and must be treated as such.' The response online was mixed. Many still believed it wasn't a direct slur towards gay men or any group other than Chelsea players. It was, and is to some, a football chant that takes on no social responsibility.

Liverpool picked up on the incident. With the club set to face Chelsea at Anfield for the first home fixture of the season the following weekend, they decided they needed to send their own message. After arriving at Kirkby, Amann waited patiently, an empty chair next to him and a microphone sound check complete. In between preparing to meet Klopp, Virgil van Dijk popped his head into the room to show solidarity with him and the community.

After a short while, Klopp emerged in his usual tracksuit. He was wide-eyed and engaging. Relaxed but eager to ensure that his terminology in his second language was correct. He checked this with Amann before the cameras rolled and they began chatting.

'I thought, "Yes," let's look at it as a chance to tell the story and appeal to the best self-image of what Liverpool is,' Amann says. 'Those values are that we show solidarity, care and have a real mutuality to each other. We did everything in one take because it was a real conversation for both of us. There wasn't much left for the cutting room.'

Throughout, Klopp cuts a composed and informed figure. He's engaged and forthright: 'It's from no perspective the nicest song in the world. It is unnecessary. It obviously makes people uncomfortable in our own fan group,' he said.

As both chatted, it was re-emphasised that the chant serves only to anger and ostracise sections of Liverpool's own supporter group rather than hindering the performance of an opposing player. That Gilmour or anyone else should not be subjected to it goes without saying, but it's also an act of complete self-sabotage.

For Liverpool and Klopp this is the antithesis of what he's built his success on. That said, it's impossible to imagine that his motive for showing solidarity is purely a matter of matchday performances. Other cynical views – that the club put him up to the interview, that he delves too much into social matters, that he has a didactic tone that intimidates those who believe he should 'stick to football'– can also be quashed. By all accounts, Klopp spoke about the matter because he believed it to be wrong and that it served no purpose to the common good of people's lives – especially those supporting his club.

Amann reflects:

> If the manager is to get the 12th man on board, they have to be more than a technician. Jürgen is an incredibly well-matched guy to what our city wants to be about. He appeals to the best version of Liverpool as it sees itself. He energises the crowd in a way that gives you an extra one or two per cent you need to be successful on and off the pitch. He's got a very clear moral compass which isn't over-encumbered with a philosophy of something being a token gesture of the right thing to do.

The right thing to do isn't always the easiest thing to speak about. Klopp has ventured into topics on homophobia, religion and politics, in a way others wouldn't dare. The role of a football manager again becomes about the unwritten rule of solidarity at Liverpool.

Sir Kenny Dalglish became so overcome by the trauma of Hillsborough that it was said he could barely get dressed in the morning. He attended funeral after funeral for the victims and was a figurehead for the grief of the city. In the end it became too much, even for someone who loves Liverpool as much as he does. Dalglish is an extreme example. His role was one no manager should ever have been put in, and hopefully never has to hold again. But he does exemplify the nature of the responsibility that comes with the position.

Many managers are happy to abide by the terms laid out in their contract of employment as head of football operations or head coach. They would probably ask for a new press officer if it was suggested to them that the day's agenda included sitting down with LGBTQ+ fan group after a homophobic chant from your own supporters at the weekend.

For Amann, the chant brought on feelings of isolation when met with an eerie silence from those he shares commonalities with. He recalls being at Anfield for the return of Fernando Torres in Chelsea colours at the back end of the 2011/12 campaign. He'd attended with his friend, who was also gay. Both were on the Kop when it erupted in the chant aimed at the former Anfield hero.

'Earlier in the match, we'd had that warm embrace of "You'll Never Walk Alone", and that unifying sense of spurring our team on together, and suddenly it was like a huge element of crowd were saying "you don't count anymore" at us. That was a slap in the face. A bucket of water being thrown over me. Whether people realise it or not, it really is offensive.'

Amann went on a mission to talk about the impact of the chant. He spoke on fan media platforms and found other avenues to try to educate people. One of those was with Spirit of Shankly. He mentions that there was some initial resistance encountered, relating people's perceived lack of malice in intention, but the more he explained, the more he felt people understood:

> I've never had an individual fan tell me, 'No, Paul, you're wrong,' because when you break down and explain, they all understand why it's offensive to myself and other LGBTQ+ fans. They get that whether it was meant or not, what matters is ownership and dealing with the fact.
>
> I think our politics have gotten sharply meaner and nastier since the referendum. The previous Prime Minister [Boris Johnson] and previous US President [Donald Trump] greenlighted a lot of hurtful and

offensive behaviour which was homophobic because of past actions.

It's also like the pandemic allowed people to forget about some of the better social norms which have previously applied. I don't think it's a coincidence that Liverpool had a raft of homophobic, transphobic hate crimes in our city centre in 2021. It felt like there wasn't a week going by without someone being left battered, bloodied and bruised on our city streets.

The attacks in question came that summer, when a slow easing of lockdown laws led to a spate of violent attacks on people in the LGBTQ+ community in the city centre. One of those men, Josh Bowen, was attacked in the early hours of 17 June. 'It's 2021, things are supposed to be better for us now,' he told BBC's *Newsbeat*.

Merseyside Police quickly recognised the matter. Superintendent Sarah Kenwright stated in a press conference: 'The incidents we have seen in the city in recent weeks have understandably caused anger and some fear among those communities targeted with homophobic and transphobic abuse. It is heartening to see so many speak in solidarity with the victims, and to say with a united voice that such behaviour simply has no place in Merseyside.'

On 22 June a protest took place in the city against the attacks. It was heavily attended in solidarity and support of the LGBTQ+ community. Newly elected mayor Joanne Anderson was present and described Liverpool as a 'proud, welcoming and inclusive city' before adding that 'hate is not welcome here'.

That theme echoed across the city, and incidents have largely remained down since last summer. Although a problem on its own patch, so to speak, it's important to recognise that this wasn't an issue solely responsible to and from people in the city. At least one of the men charged with the attacks came from a different town or city in the North West.

The parade showed a public display of resolve – Liverpool remains a bastion of resistance. During a planned protest from the English Defence League (EDL) in the city in 2017, anti-fascist groups and ordinary people from the city stood firm against the spread of hate-filled propaganda. Together, they met the group with a sea of red flares and a unified chorus of 'fuck off'. The EDL quickly U-turned back to Lime Street station, accompanied by the Benny Hill theme music booming out across St George's Hall.

The general mood music of Liverpool maintains the rhythm of inclusion that runs through the city. Like football, taking your cue from the macro instead of the micro is usually the best way to judge actions for yourself. If you sit next to one person at Anfield whose actions you don't particularly like, but the overwhelming majority of the Kop stands to applaud the Manchester United goalkeeper as he runs towards them, which one is more representative of collective behaviour? Unfortunately, the actions of a single person can often be just as long-lasting.

For Klopp this comes down to addressing and confronting behaviours and attitudes he doesn't want to see in life, society and football. His actions have undoubtedly gone hand-in-hand with the stand Liverpool has taken on the issues of discrimination against the LGBTQ+ community.

Prior to his interview with Amann, he sat with Liverpool Women's footballer Meikayla Moore to discuss representation in the game and the Rainbow Laces campaign. Moore asked Klopp what he thought of the campaign and understanding of LGBTQ+, the Liverpool manager paused before directing attention towards the laces in his Adidas trainers:

> You should try it [rainbow laces], it feels great. And you can increase awareness of something which is really important. Because that's the problem and it's difficult. I'm 54, I went through a lot of periods in

my life. There were a lot of problems I never had, so it means you talk about it like an interested viewer. But I have so many gay friends, at my age now, and I never thought about how it was when they had to say, 'By the way, mum, dad, whoever else ... I'm not exactly how you expected it, maybe.' And that's the challenge we should not face in the way we face it in our lives.

Klopp's gesture towards rainbow laces was far from tokenism. He wore the laces throughout most of the season and continued to do so again the following one. Jordan Henderson, it must be noted, also shared a seemingly authentic response to the campaign, replying to a heartfelt message on Twitter from a Liverpool supporter after he posted himself wearing a rainbow armband.

A tweeted response from the Liverpool captain read: 'You'll Never Walk Alone, Keith. If wearing the #RainbowLaces armband helps even just one person then it's progress. Everyone is welcome at Liverpool Football Club. Hope you enjoyed the game tonight. #YNWA.'

Henderson was also swift in praising the first openly gay footballer, Adelaide United's Josh Cavallo, who he called 'courageous'. These actions would later form part of why his acrimonious move to Saudi Arabia – a place where it remains illegal to be gay – hurt many within the community, including Amann.

The appointment of someone like Tony Barrett at Liverpool – a Scouser who covered the club extensively and with considered decency and insight over many years – shows that getting the right people in the right places matters. This is something Klopp has championed in his modest observations about his management philosophy. 'Have strong people around you with better knowledge in different departments than yourself,' Klopp told the club website in an interview with

Western Union in 2019. 'Don't act like you know everything and be ready to admit that. It's not a real philosophy, it's just my way of life. If I would expect I know everything and I'm the best at everything, I couldn't have confidence, but I don't expect that.'

If Liverpool's general improvement in inclusivity is marked, it's also important to mention what they haven't done well on Klopp's watch, even if it's not something he has any direct or daily involvement in. The most glaring was the treatment of Liverpool FC Women. The fall of the team since their first FA Women's Super League title in 2013 was heavy and reached its nadir six years later when the club was relegated from the top flight. Their plummet was marred by criticism from exiting players, who felt there was no real commitment from the club to develop and build women's football. A perceived neglectful lack of investment was emphasised by the new training facility at Kirkby, which opened in November 2020 and had no committed space for its female squad.

Although the club had a committed to a deal with local League Two club Tranmere Rovers to host women's fixtures at their Prenton Park stadium on the Wirral, the sense of isolation prevailed. FSG committed more resources to getting Liverpool Women back to where they should be. Increased coverage from local fan groups and journalists also shone a light on developments there.

In September 2023 Liverpool Women moved into their new base of operations at Melwood, following the club's investment in regenerating the previous training ground and making it a purpose-built hub for the team. This was in time for the new season, after Liverpool Women sealed the Championship title, ensuring a top-flight return, to the delight of Klopp, who was keen to celebrate and quick to acknowledge past wrongdoings:

> I've been following it all the time. I was always looking at the results after our games, around our

games, looking when they play, who they play. After the result from last week it was clear with a draw against Bristol they could make it, and they won. Really happy for the girls, and for Matt. It's a big, big thing.

Obviously, Liverpool was, in the last years, not famous for treating or dealing with women's football outstandingly well. They didn't go down to the Championship for no reason. But now they are back and now we have to make sure that we use the situation.

I met a lot of the girls in the last two or three months for different reasons, did wonderful stuff together with Meikayla [Moore] for LGBT, which was really great, then I spoke to others. It's really nice. To be honest, it's a wonderful team, great coach and I'm really happy for them to get promoted.

Like every action Klopp has taken with Liverpool's LGBTQ+ community – and, in fact, everything that matters so much to all supporters – everything has a reason, everything has substance, and everything is for the good of those impacted to improve togetherness and inclusion.

Part 3

Champions

Chapter 9

Our Year

THERE'S A certain list of terminology in football's banter-derived guidebook reserved for Liverpool. Like every global superpower in football, Liverpool are loved and hated with equal passion.

Success spanning across the 1970s and 80s was barely tolerable to rival supporters. But combined with passionate romanticism and the republican tendencies of the club's supporter base, fans of other clubs have felt pushed to the limits of their endurance. Whether from jealousy or simple rivalry, the tag of 'unbearable' has been attached to Liverpool fans and the threat of trophy success, especially a long-awaited league title.

It's perhaps a sign of how football, like politics and other areas of society, has become increasingly extremist and tribal. While a bit of competitiveness is one thing, the use of hate as a descriptor is now routinely applied without any room for compassion. Paradoxically, football has always been a place where both heartless cruelty and human decency can exist in the same vehicle.

Under Klopp, a new generation of supporter has come of age. But this also meant that a new cohort, with different cultural experiences, faced the increased poverty chants and tragedy taunting. The better Klopp's Liverpool became, the more others seemed to loath them.

Jordi Holden is a 23-year-old Liverpool fan from the city. Holden didn't miss a single fixture of the club's 64-match run in 2021/22, which almost resulted in an unprecedented quadruple. He says:

> I have always personally loved the statement 'hated all over England, adored all over Europe', which is what we truly are when we go abroad visiting different countries with Liverpool.
>
> I think this has been enhanced since Klopp's arrival and his presence that is felt and admired throughout European football. The stigmas and stereotypes you hear from other fans in England, even those as close as across a park in Everton, all seem to go away when interacting with different cultures and supporters abroad.
>
> I personally thought Inter Milan and Villarreal treated us with the most respect during 21/22. Villarreal especially because they had so much admiration for us and couldn't believe they were in a European Cup semi-final; swapping scarfs afterwards with their ultras was a good thing to see.

If 'The Unbearables', as Liverpool had been rebranded in 2019, were to live up to their latest moniker, they had to eradicate another phrase that had been used as a stick to beat them for 30 years. 'It's our year' is how opposition fans chose to mock the Reds' anguishing quest for a 19th league title. Plenty attributed the term to a sense of entitlement or, worse, delusion.

Liverpool is a massive club; such expectancy had substance and had to come from somewhere. When it wasn't met, frustration naturally grew into despair. The glee found in that particular trophy drought was itself unbearable to most Liverpool fans.

Was it a fantastical expectation for Liverpool, despite drifting further from what had become such routine success with each passing year since 1991? Success was by no means delivered regularly, but Liverpool were never without big moments. There was never a prolonged sense they were *that* far away.

Liverpool FC journalist and correspondent Neil Jones recalls:

> I remember speaking to Phil Thompson during the coronavirus lockdown, 2020, and something he said really struck me. He said he never ever went into a season thinking that Liverpool couldn't win the league, whether he was playing, [assistant] managing or just watching as a fan: 'I always thought we just had to get on a roll and get things together and we'd be alright. Even when Manchester United were at their best, or Arsenal or Chelsea, I always thought it'd be our year.'
>
> Don't you think that's mad? I mean, doesn't that show just how big an effect Liverpool's period of dominance had, how much it fostered this sense of belief, almost delusion and entitlement?
>
> 'It's their year' became a joke to rival fans, but I think it started from Liverpudlians, and I think they usually believed it at the time too. Never mind the logic, think of the badge. It'll all be okay. A new signing here, a bit of momentum there, and it'll be our year, just like it always used to be.

By the time Klopp arrived, expectation had turned to desperation in some parts – and resignation in others. Liverpool had suffered in their quest for league glory, most notably in 2008/09 under Benítez, and again in 2013/14 with Rodgers. There were those who even began to investigate the legitimacy of a supposed curse on the part of former goalkeeper Bruce Grobbelaar, and his links to a South African witch doctor. Legend had it that on Grobbelaar's testimonial in 1992, a witch doctor from his latest sponsor Zambezi lager was sent to Anfield and weaved a wicked spell.

'He [the witch doctor] went around on the posts and put his goat's tail, put his water on the posts of both sides, got the microphone and said, "If you don't have the jungle man Bruce Grobbelaar here, you won't win the title,"' said Grobbelaar in an interview with BT Sport in 2019.

Grobbelaar had attempted to reverse the hex with the only known remedy: by urinating on all four home goalposts. He made it to the Kop after a charity match in the 2013/14 season but was stopped before he could get to the Anfield Road end. In another match in 2019, he took a bottle of his own urine, disguised as a water bottle, and finished the job.

As Liverpool entered their fourth full season under Klopp, talk of cursed spells and mocking chants were very much subsiding. A year after the disappointment of Kyiv, Klopp had created a team built to compete at the highest level. He needed it. Liverpool and Manchester City relentlessly went into battle with one another, each aiming to secure a title during what would arguably go down as one of the most prime-quality modern rivalries in Premier League history.

In 2018/19 Liverpool furnished themselves with a world-class goalkeeper in Alisson Becker. By the end of his debut season, he'd won the Champions League, three Golden Gloves, and the Copa América for Brazil. Along with the arrival of Van Dijk in January 2017, Alisson allowed Klopp to employ a more aggressive press; although this used advanced numbers and left gaps behind, this luxury security at the back meant it would be reliably swept up.

Liverpool would often line up on TV monitors and team sheets in what looked like a familiar 4-3-3, although it was anything but. Fabinho – brought in a day after defeat in Ukraine for £40m from Monaco – was described by Lijnders as Liverpool's 'lighthouse', keeping watch and constantly sniffing out danger before it happened. He was perfect for what the system required from the single pivot, or 'six' as Klopp often positionally describes it. Nimble Red Bull Leipzig midfielder Naby Keïta had finally come in, showing snippets of his undoubted ability and promising a lot more.

Such was the development in players such as Alexander-Arnold and Robertson at full-back – who would go on to post 16 and 13 assists respectively that season – that Liverpool often looked more like a 2-3-5 or 2-4-4 shape in possession. They were better at patiently probing and building attacking patterns in these shapes. Guardiola's Manchester City were still the masters of this, but Klopp was slowly adding it to his team's repertoire of competencies.

Two grinding early-season wins came at Leicester and Tottenham in consecutive fixtures. This was topped off by a scintillating late 3-2 win over PSG at Anfield, which showed a grittier relentlessness than many had seen before.

By the time Divock Origi made a gamble on a ball falling on to the Kop crossbar in the 96th minute of added time in a Merseyside derby, or Xherdan Shaqiri had a blitzing cameo in the rain against Manchester United, and Roberto Firmino was fashioning stills worthy of being hung in the Albert Dock's Tate Gallery after a hat-trick against Arsenal, the belief that a title challenge was legitimate was impossible to deny.

It was the derby winner that had everyone energised, including Jamie Carragher's quest to hold himself together in Sky's commentary box after Origi's goal, bursting with 'look at Jürgen Klopp!' as the German sprinted on to the pitch and into the arms of his goalkeeper. Klopp knew what a derby goal meant, but he also knew it fed back to the Crystal Palace and West Brom days in 2015. If he could get the crowd to stay until the end, anything could be possible. Liverpool had belief and momentum; he also knew what that could do.

City beat Liverpool in a nerve-shredding match at the Etihad on 3 January 2019 thanks to a Leroy Sané strike not long after one of the most exquisitely worked goals a Klopp team has produced to equalise. Moving City all over the pitch with 14 carefully constructed passes, the ball ended up at Firmino's head to tap in. But it wasn't enough, and the match would be best remembered for the 1.12 centimetres that denied a ball crossing the line of City's goal, and a red card not given to Vincent Kompany for a reckless lunge on Salah.

In the first few months of the New Year, Liverpool drew four of six league encounters, including two forgetful 0-0 stalemates at Old Trafford and Goodison Park. They wouldn't drop another league point after Everton, but neither would City – a final tally of 97 points would be agonisingly short on the final day, with Guardiola's men reaching 98 after a win at Brighton, despite falling behind.

Liverpool had equipped themselves to compete on all fronts. They'd overcome a last-16 Champions League tie with Bayern Munich, putting on a display of resolve and tenacity by winning 3-1 at The Allianz following a 0-0 first leg at Anfield.

'They [Bayern] knew this was a different cup of tea tonight. This is a big, big step for us. We set a mark for this wonderful club that we really are back on the landscape of top football,' Klopp said after the match.

Klopp was animated on a personal level on the touchline. He had history with Bayern for years at both Dortmund and Mainz, living in the shadow of German football's darling. For years they imposed themselves on his aspirations. Now he had a powerhouse of his own, which remained in his own image. He had the passion, the quality and the will to press on and deliver silverware. And he'd just brushed them aside in the biggest competition of all.

'This club [Bayern] always has outstandingly strong football teams, they have one now. I really think this club [Liverpool] deserves awareness again. We are back, and I like this fact,' he said with an unmitigated degree of *schadenfreude* attached.

Klopp's development as a coach and leader was to face its ultimate test on Tuesday, 7 May 2019. Liverpool were due to host Barcelona, and the Reds were 3-0 down from a first leg that was littered with such a degree of admirable opposition quality that they were fortunate not to have conceded one or two more.

In the first leg, Henderson and Firmino were left on the bench, with Wijnaldum occupying the false-nine role. Despite starting well, the home team created opportunities by working the channels behind Liverpool's advancing full-backs. Suárez was in a particularly devilish mood, to the surprise of some Reds fans; his simulation, referee protestation and celebration was par for the course, yet his aggression towards Robertson wouldn't be forgotten.

When Liverpool piled bodies forward to snatch a crucial away goal in the dying moments, Barcelona broke and looked certain to make it four. Ousmane Dembélé had the goal at his mercy from around 12 yards but blazed over. The reaction of Lionel Messi was telling. He looked as though his team-mate had squandered the chance to win the tie completely, despite the already formidable lead.

Liverpool had no time for self-deprecation, as they travelled to a feral Newcastle United at 5.30pm the following Saturday, between the two Barcelona ties. The Reds won via more Origi heroics in the dying minutes, but lost Salah to a concussion. Firmino was also ruled out of the return tie with Barcelona.

To put it bluntly, Liverpool were a lame duck in the eyes of most. The second leg was being set up as a procession for the visitors. Suárez and Coutinho posed for pictures in Anfield and spoke warmly of their former home the day before. It had a testimonial feel to the watching world.

Klopp later described what he told his players before going out:

> 'We have to play without two of the best strikers in the world. The world outside is saying it is not possible. And let's be honest, it's probably impossible. But because it's you? Because it's you, we have a chance.'

I really believed that. It wasn't about their technical ability as footballers. It was about who they were as human beings, and everything they had overcome in life. The only thing that I added was: 'If we fail, then let's fail in the most beautiful way.'

If the players already believed it, the crowd were soon on board too after Origi struck on seven minutes. Robertson would physically impose himself, let's say, on a shell-shocked Messi. Fabinho cleanly left a mark on the Reds' former No.7, activating the vengeful humour of the Kop with a chant of 'fuck off, Suárez' on repeat. This felt like a far cry from clapping a chauvinistic Cristiano Ronaldo off the Anfield turf. After a 3-1 defeat to Real Madrid in 2014, that was a rare act of unworthy appreciation and a depiction of just how lost Liverpool were.

It was the collective will and purpose that clawed Liverpool back from the brink against Barcelona. Alisson made crucial stops, Wijnaldum seemed to use his frustration at not starting to score twice, and Salah championed from the sidelines in his 'Never Give Up' embroidered T-shirt.

Liverpool had pulled off a seemingly impossible 4-0 win over 90 minutes against a team laden with star quality. Two goals from Origi added to Wijnaldum's brace – the last from a quick Alexander-Arnold corner that dumbfounded a shell-shocked, unprepared Barcelona. Anfield erupted at full time. Younger supporters I'd been reassuring around me fell into a tornado of bodily exhaustion and jubilation, immersed in one another with adoration and tears of unbelievable joy. A young ball boy exceeded the terms of his job role by sprinting on to the pitch towards his heroes, leaving the iconic image of flipping a V-sign at chasing stewards. The ultimate act of Scouse defiance, as some later labelled it.

Liverpool fan Damian Kavanagh was there. Having followed the club since the 1980s, he suggests: 'Liverpool is

European football royalty, there's no doubt about that; and Klopp knew he could make that [Liverpool's European status] another player. When Barcelona came for the second leg, I knew there was only one postcode which could deliver that miracle, it was L4 0TH.'

Jonathan Wilson's piece in *The Guardian* the following day cited Barcelona's possession game as the key factor in their elimination. The piece alluded to the idea that Liverpool's aggression was now too much for the Johan Cruyff-inspired doctrine for how the beautiful game *should* be played. An important caveat is that Liverpool weren't the villains of this piece, they were heroes. They were the antithesis of the (perhaps unfairly labelled) defensive, time-wasting, smash-and-grab teams that Houllier and Benítez had previously managed.

It had become impossible for anyone to live with Liverpool on their day. They had too much nous, an indefatigable work ethic and a wealth of technical brilliance. Klopp had evolved fundamental parts of his Mainz and Dortmund identities to develop the complete package at Liverpool. He knew in the quiet after the storm of Barcelona that he'd come full circle, but the job wasn't over. He said later:

> When I got to my little boot room after the match, I didn't even have a sip of beer. I didn't need it. I sat there with a bottle of water in silence, just smiling. It was a feeling that I cannot describe in words. When I got back home, my family and friends were all staying over at our house, and everyone was in a big party mood. But I was so emotionally exhausted that I went up to bed by myself. My body and mind were completely empty. I had the best sleep of my life.

To be in Madrid for Liverpool's second Champions League Final in as many years will stoke memories of sweltering heat, and Webster's guitar-riff choreography in the fan park at

Plaza Felipe II to around 50,000 of the club's fans. The most memorable moment was his stoic rendition of Van Dijk's chant to the tune of 'Dirty Old Town' by The Pogues.

'I saw that video before pre-match [of the final],' the Dutchman said later in an interview with Jones. 'I couldn't sleep anymore. I just wanted to get out there. I don't have that [feeling] too much, I was ready to go. I wanted to go out there, get the trophy and party with them as well.'

Liverpool simply wouldn't be denied this time around; Klopp's reputation as being a loser of big finals would finally come to an end. After securing an early 1-0 lead through a Salah penalty, the scoreline persisted for most of the tie against Mauricio Pochettino's Tottenham. That is, until Origi doubled their advantage late on from the bench to showcase his knack for a big occasion. Klopp wasn't about to let any of the moment escape him. Liverpool had the trophy they deserved after taking City to the brink domestically. If they couldn't be league champions, they should rightly be crowned six-time European kings.

They hadn't relied on a sense of fate to seal their own. The manager and his staff had prepared for Tottenham with a secret match arranged by Klopp, Lijnders and other members of the backroom team. Perceptively, they'd realised similarities between Benfica's B team and Tottenham, so they were given a specific brief to mirror Tottenham's attacking and defensive movements and the patterns that Liverpool anticipated they would use.

'We recreated two of their offensive and two of their defensive moments, as well as the set pieces we thought they'd use in the final,' manager Renato Paiva said. 'We replicated their centre-back and goalkeeper build-up routines, their 4-2-3-1 defensive shape with the striker cutting between opposition centre-backs and the 10 obstructing Liverpool's 6. Vinícius mimicked [Christian] Eriksen, Bernardo acted more like [Dele] Alli and José Gomes was [Harry] Kane.'

Liverpool and Klopp had learned from the defeat in Kyiv. They also had the ability to put on a show without any fireworks. This was a Champions League Final completely on their terms, far from the one-trick pony of heavy-metal football many had perceived Klopp to be.

I was in Madrid; I'd been in Kyiv the year before. Both were lifetime trips in their own right, but Spain had been particularly, well, wholesome. Travelling into Madrid, and enjoying wine and tapas with friends, I was so calmly certain that Liverpool were about to win one of the biggest matches in football. You could argue a certain arrogance to that, but the team had learned so much from the previous 12 months and I'd learned watching them. They were ready to win something big. As ready as I'd ever known anything.

The next day, 'Old Big Ears', as it's known in the city, was paraded around the streets of Liverpool, culminating in a stunning display along the Strand, a stretch of road running parallel to its picturesque waterfront. For Klopp and many of his players, turning on to that stretch of road gave them corroboration, if needed, of the sheer magnitude of the club. Klopp later said:

> I have no words that can describe the emotions of that day. We were riding in the bus, and every time we thought the parade had to be over – that there could not possibly be any more people in the city of Liverpool – we would turn a corner and the parade would go on. Absolutely unreal. If you could've put all the emotions, all the excitement, all the love in the air that day and bottled it up, the world would be a better place.
>
> I have not been able to get the emotion of that day out of my head. Football has given me everything in my life. But I really want to do more to give back to the world. Easy for me to say, okay. Sure. But how do you actually make a difference?

His urge to contribute and make a difference was put into action in September 2019, when he joined Common Goal – a charity working towards cultural and social solutions, funded by members, like Klopp, who donate one per cent of their annual income to its cause. He said on announcing his allegiance:

> How can you not feel inspired by this? This is what football is all about. I just want to be a part of this. So, I'm pledging one per cent of my yearly salary to Common Goal, and I hope that many, many more people in the football world will join me. Let's be honest, guys. We are extremely fortunate. It is our responsibility as privileged people to give something back to children all over the world who just need a chance in life.
>
> We should not forget what it was like when we had real problems. This bubble we live in is not the real world. I am sorry, but anything that happens on a football pitch is not a real problem. There should be a bigger purpose to this game than revenue and trophies, no? Just think what we could accomplish if we all came together and gave one per cent of what we earn to make a positive difference in the world. Maybe I am naive. Maybe I am a crazy old dreamer. But who is this game for? We all know damn well that this game is for dreamers.

Klopp may not have taken his last line directly from a Liverpool-inspired songbook, but he had a team, club and city in a dreamland of their own – one they could hardly imagine. There was only one thing left: the holy grail. This wasn't Liverpool's year on the domestic front, but there was a feeling that it was now only a matter of time.

Chapter 10

The Hurt

THERE'S NO way of immersing yourself in Liverpool Football Club without feeling the devastation of the Hillsborough tragedy – a day when 95 Liverpool fans lost their lives due to organisational failures by stadium staff and South Yorkshire Police in Sheffield on 15 April 1989.

Tony Bland became the 96th supporter to die, in 1993, as a result of brain damage caused by asphyxia on the day. Andrew Devine died in July 2021, becoming the 97th victim, as a result of his life-changing injuries. Around Anfield, Hillsborough's presence can be felt beyond the eternal flame memorial on the Main Stand side. It was an event that became one of the most defining moments since the club's birth in 1892, and remains so.

'Hillsborough is something which changed Liverpool Football Club forever,' Damian Kavanagh recalls. He's a survivor who was in the Leppings Lane end where the crush occurred that day. 'And because the club is so intrinsically linked to its people and history, it changed the city forever. It will always be synonymous with the hurt, the pain and the injustice. And then the pride, love and standing up for what's right.'

It would change the trajectory of the club in every way. Many who now associate Liverpool with an entrenched anti-establishment mind – or a 'victim complex' as Boris Johnson would describe the city, before later issuing a grovelling, unaccepted apology – do so with a cowardly Hillsborough narrative implicitly or explicitly attached.

Four days after the tragedy, *The Sun* newspaper ran the headline: 'The Truth'. It depicted supporters as people who not only caused the incident through being late and drunk, but as people who stole from and urinated on the dead. It was beyond inhumane, despicable, and will never be forgotten.

This was only part of the smear. The bereaved families, with all of Liverpool's collective support, had to face a fight for justice against the authorities in charge. It would officially last until 2016, when the cause of 'accidental death' was ruled incorrect by a damning report from an independent panel reviewing the case. The victims' families had already lived through unimaginable anguish; the survivors were left with their own trauma and an entire city was left numb with pain.

'You could taste the sorrow in the air,' Kavanagh says. 'It affected everyone and everything. I remember a local DJ on a random Radio City show not long after it happened ending the show by saying "chin up". I think we all know what he meant. It changed me. My life is pre-Hillsborough and post-Hillsborough in the same way it's pre-fatherhood and post-fatherhood. The first disaster was the event, the second disaster was the cover-up.'

Despite the long-overdue verdict, justice was still not delivered, as key figure Chief Superintendent and Match Commander David Duckenfield was found not guilty of gross negligence manslaughter at a retrial on 28 November 2019. It was an ordeal the families described as 'like being back in 1991', due to accusations of falsely proven blame on Liverpool supporters resurfacing during the trial. Norman Bettison, a South Yorkshire police inspector at the time who later became Chief Constable of Merseyside Police, was charged with misconduct in a public office – but that trial collapsed in 2018.

David Conn, who covered Hillsborough extensively for *The Guardian*, wrote about the cover-up in 2021:

> The lies began even as people were dying. The police officer in command, Ch Supt David Duckenfield,

failed to take control of the chaos and organise a concerted rescue operation, but he started the false narrative that would form the foundation of enduring injustice. In an episode still profoundly shocking decades on, at 3.15pm Duckenfield lied to the Football Association official, Graham Kelly, telling him that Liverpool supporters had forced open a gate, and rushed into the Leppings Lane end of the ground.

That story was given to the media at 3.25pm. John Motson reported in a live BBC broadcast that a gate was said to have been broken down, and that non-ticket holders had forced their way in. As recently as the 2022 Champions League Final, such a narrative was chillingly familiar. As a result of the actions of police at the Stade de France, a similar situation seemed only narrowly avoided because of the incredible restraint and maturity shown by Liverpool supporters locked outside the stadium, despite arriving with plenty of time and with genuine tickets.

In Paris, supporters were filmed horded into narrow passageways. As they arrived at the stadium, police action became more unnecessarily robust. The use of tear gas was employed in response to people asking for help, concerned for their own welfare. These people had lived with this their entire lives. They'd attended a football match – paying a lot of money to do so – and their safety was now in danger through no fault of their own. A message from inside the stadium went straight to an unverified explanation that fans turning up late had caused the delay in kick-off. Television network BT Sport did nothing to challenge this and establish the facts during their live coverage. Fortunately, access to camera phones and the sheer number of people from press, sponsors, players' and staff families, and corporate guests quickly voiced what had actually happened, to eradicate any suggestion that Liverpool supporters were responsible. Their reach would be vital to ensure another cover-up couldn't take place.

UEFA and the French authorities continued to peddle uncorroborated and unsubstantiated claims linked to Liverpool supporters. The most desperate of these came from Gérald Darmanin – France's Interior Minister – who, without proof, claimed that 40,000 fake tickets were in operation at Liverpool-allocated entrance points, which caused the delay. He would later backtrack and apologise as well as be proven factually incorrect. UEFA's head of events stated that around 2,600 fake tickets were known to be in circulation. 'Should the Stade de France have been better managed? The answer is yes,' he told the French radio station RTL around a month after the event. Darmanin faced no punishment.

Inarguable facts of what transpired on the night narrowly avoided another cover-up in 2022, but those from 1989 still live with Hillsborough's injustice. Right away the victims were being blamed for their own deaths and injuries. South Yorkshire Police Chief Constable Peter Wright admitted hours later that Gate C, which had played a huge role in the tragedy, had not been forced but that Duckenfield himself had given the order for it to be opened, sending innocent supporters into already overcrowded pens.

The families' collective resilience was what led to the inquest eventually being reopened. They opened with accounts from family members of victims. Steve Kelly, who lost his older brother Michael, described his sibling as 'our Mike' and someone who was more than just a number. 'I've come here to reclaim him,' he told the court.

Thirty-seven teenagers had died. Twenty-five of those who died were fathers: 58 people lost a parent. Three babies were born after their fathers died at Hillsborough.

'Many survivors came as witnesses; they included off-duty police officers, doctors and nurses, and the humanity of the people who suffered made the police portrayal of them as an out-of-control mob look cruel, and evidently false,' wrote Conn in the same piece.

From the outset, the cover-up around Hillsborough was an attack on a place and a social class. A place where skilled, smart and valued people with hope of a future went to a game of football and lost their lives through no fault of their own.

Kavanagh says:

> I've got to where I am because of the love and support around me as well as the knowledge that not only did we do nothing wrong, we were in the right. It was hard to talk about. I only wrote my account [years later for the Hillsborough Justice Campaign] because I thought of my son and what he would wonder about me when I'm gone. I started to think my voice wasn't important. Then I thought about what it would be like if my grandchildren read *The Sun*. I would climb out of my grave.
>
> Would the Nottingham Forest fans be besmirched the way we were if it'd been them? Would they carry on the campaign the way we would? There's no way to answer this, so in that sense the tragedy stays with us.

Liverpool are now more subjected to Hillsborough chanting than ever before. Rival fans across the country have sung 'always the victims, it's never your fault' with increasing decibel levels the more successful Liverpool have become under Klopp. Both Manchester City and Manchester United crowds have been heard to mercilessly chant: '*The Sun* was right, you're murderers.'

Nobody talks about the real issues: what this says about the state of football. What chants like that do to the survivors and family members. Why anyone thinks this is somehow tribalised and part of 'the banter'. For an increasing majority, these abhorrent chants have become the only way to claim any kind of victory over Liverpool. But this cruelty and inconsiderate hate has no place at all in football or society. Klopp himself acknowledged the clear chanting heard from opposing fans across the country in his programme notes that followed the 33rd anniversary:

> Really? The deaths of 97 people in a tragedy is now something that can be mocked? How did this happen? We have staff at the club who lost loved ones at Hillsborough. There are supporters in the crowd at all of our games who lost friends or family members themselves or who survived the tragedy. They have already suffered more than enough. No one should think it is okay to make them suffer more because it absolutely is not. So I will say this very clearly: if you are going to a football match to sing about people losing their lives you really should not bother coming.

A case of defence, usually from faceless social media accounts, often points to denial from Liverpool to acknowledge the Heysel Stadium disaster in which 39 supporters lost their lives when a fence was forced during the European Cup Final between Liverpool and Juventus. This is usually coupled with a plain ignorance that Hillsborough was something that could, and should, have been avoided. It could have been any other set of supporters that day, and might be so again.

In its own way, this further works to exonerate Duckenfield, Bettison and the wider establishment, and that creates a more insular and distrusting Liverpool. There's no doubt it still shapes the city and football club in every sense. With every mocking chant to the deaths of 97 people, the sheer injustice that lingers from Hillsborough will churn and regurgitate.

Dalglish became a vessel of support for the families in the immediate aftermath, at one point attending four funerals in one day with wife, Marina. It would eventually and unsurprisingly take its toll on him. 'You never ever forget what happened. But if it was difficult for us, imagine what the families are going through, they sacrificed their lives,' he said.

Dalglish was modest, caring and selfless. He saw it as his duty to be there for the people: 'If, sometimes, you put someone else before yourself, I don't know what's wrong with that. As far as we were concerned, we were fortunate our damage was not as permanent as it was for the families. If we were damaged for a little bit, then fine. For the help that we gave to the people who most needed it at that time, it's a small price to pay.'

But at home he was restless, irritable and exhausted. Marina described him as 'terrible to live with' during that time. He was taking sleeping pills and broke out in shingles. While all of this was happening, the job of managing England's most successful club turned inexorably, like the hands of a clock. Dalglish delivered the title in 1990/91 – the last until Klopp's arrival – but quit after a 4-4 derby with Everton, 21 months after Hillsborough, when he found himself hesitating over in-match decisions. 'If I cannae make decisions, I don't deserve to be there,' he later said.

Kavanagh suggests:

> Nobody's ever talked about how the disaster impacted Liverpool's success. I couldn't believe in 1991 people were questioning why Kenny wanted to quit. I wanted to quit.
>
> Kenny needed a break, had one, came back and won the league with Blackburn Rovers. But [him leaving] wasn't the only reason. Liverpool had a hell of a run with the boot room philosophy, and that may have come to its natural end, but there's no doubt [Hillsborough] impacted what Liverpool did on the pitch. That was the least of my concern at the time.
>
> The truth was that nobody was ready to continue with life as they'd once known it. I found the start

of the next season difficult; it was like, 'Oh, am I supposed to be okay now?' Mental health back then still meant having a stiff upper lip as most families were carrying a post-war mentality, but after [Hillsborough] I couldn't do that.

The solace I had was being in the city, in the community. I could talk directly to people who were experiencing the same as me. Everyone in work, pubs or wherever had been affected. But that also made it harder because it was me and my own people. I can't say this now, as a family man, but back then I'd have traded myself in as the Hillsborough one to stop all that pain.

Liverpool were in limbo. They were understandably unprepared for the disaster or its impact on every aspect of the club, including Dalglish's decision to quit. They would recruit the only way they knew how: internally and with one of their own.

Former captain Graeme Souness moved into Dalglish's post following a successful managerial stint in Glasgow at Rangers FC. He would be given time to integrate his own methods, but he was operating in ways that Liverpool weren't used to. Souness introduced nutrition and discipline around fitness, which, while progressive, was perhaps a little too ahead of its time for a traditionalist set-up like Liverpool's.

I was once present at a sportsman dinner where Jan Mølby was giving a speech. The former Liverpool midfielder told us that he was summoned to Souness's office on his first day back of pre-season; when asked about his lightest-ever bodyweight, the Dane replied: 'Nine pounds, three ounces, boss.'

Souness bought poorly. Players such as Julian Dicks, István Kozma and Torben Piechnik were not of the quality Liverpool required. The club finished sixth in 1992/93. The following season, attendances at Anfield were regularly under 30,000. On top of that, Souness had sold the story of his triple heart bypass to *The Sun*, a decision so staggeringly and arrogantly ill-judged it continues to defy belief.

He was replaced by Roy Evans in January 1994. The squad he inherited needed much renovation, but had young local talent coming through, which looked ripe for picking. Most notably this included Steve McManaman from Bootle and, latterly, Toxteth's own Robbie Fowler.

Football continued its attempts to recover in the aftermath of Hillsborough, and in 1992 published the Taylor Report – Lord Justice Taylor's findings and recommendations for future crowd safety. However, some measures around offences linked to alcohol consumption within sight of a football ground, which weren't implemented in other sports held at the same venues, only served to add to the conscious stereotypical links to hooliganism around the disaster, and football in general.

Taylor also recommended that all grounds in the old First and Second Divisions of the Football League (now the Premier League and League Championship) should be all-seated by August 1994, thus removing standing terraces. Taylor advised that clubs in the former Third and Fourth Divisions (current League 1 and League 2) of the English Football League should be all-seated by August 1999.

After a review of the government's all-seater policy, on 10 July 1992 the Secretary of State for National Heritage declared that clubs in the lower two divisions of the Football League could keep some standing terracing, as long as it met specific criteria and standards. Clubs in the top tiers were still required to meet the August 1994 deadline to remove standing terraces.

Anfield hosted its last match in front of the old standing Kop against Norwich City on 30 April 1994, as the Reds miserably bowed out to a 1-0 defeat. It felt as if a piece of Anfield had been taken forever, albeit for something deemed a safer cause. The symbolism of the stand was so crucial to what Liverpool was that many felt the passion would disappear with the redevelopment.

The original Kop was built in 1906. After Liverpool won their second league title, the club directors erected a new brick and cinder banking at the Walton Breck Road end of the ground to cope with the extra demand. The new mound was christened the Spion Kop, in memory of those from the city who died at a hill of the same name during the Boer War in South Africa.

On the day of its last stand, Gerry Marsden gave a rousing live rendition of 'You'll Never Walk Alone' from the centre circle. Past players were brought out to a crowd full of people overcome with emotion.

When Norwich midfielder Jeremy Goss scored the only goal of the match in 1994, he seemingly earned himself the title of last player to score in front of the Kop (despite the collective retort of 'you're supposed to let us win' from the 30,000 or so present behind the goal).

Liverpool fan John Garner wanted to etch his own name into the history books. At full time, he ran on to the pitch dressed as a Spion Kop war veteran, complete with fez, handlebar moustache, knee-length shorts and khaki army shirt to seize an opportunity to write his name into Liverpool folklore.

'Everyone refused to leave the Kop on the final whistle,' he told *The Sportsman* over two decades later. 'We wanted to stay there as long as possible, but once it became obvious that the players weren't coming out again I noticed a ball had been left in the net at our end, which one of the stewards had thrown to some kids near where I was standing.'

Garner jumped over the barrier at the front of the terrace and ran with the ball to the middle of the pitch, to the delight of a still-packed Kop, before turning and noticing a once-in-a-lifetime opportunity.

> I ran towards the goal at the Kop end and as I reached the edge of the box curled the ball into the corner, which wasn't easy when you're wearing a pair of

hobnail army boots. But before I could jump back into the Kop I was grabbed by two of Merseyside's finest police officers and marched to the Anfield Road end. Thankfully they saw the funny side of it and I was just told not to do it again and have a good night. I met up with the lads not long after and without it really sinking in what I'd done someone pointed out that I'd just scored the last goal in front of the Kop.

Liverpool lost the battle against Norwich, and there was increasing evidence they were losing the war of retaining their grip at the top of the domestic tree. In the distance, through the watchful eye of the famous old terrace, there was an army coming over the hill, marching with increasing strength, power and a leadership showing the battle-hardened qualities Liverpool were lacking.

A season after Liverpool had lifted their last title, success hinged on the more unfamiliar task of stopping Manchester United. Although they could only muster a sixth-place finish and were winless in five coming into the match, the Reds beat Alex Ferguson's momentum-gathering United 2-0, thanks to goals from Ian Rush and Mark Walters, to the delight of the home crowd. The defeat effectively handed the title to Leeds United and kept it out of reach of their Mancunian counterparts.

Stephen Armstrong originates from the Moston area of Manchester and has been an ardent United match-goer for most of his life. He was at Anfield that day: 'I always remember seeing Liverpool fans delighting in United's failure after we essentially lost the league title at Anfield in 92. A lot of United fans see that as a dark day, but for me it was a really significant moment. I felt that was the point United were passing Liverpool on the stairs.'

Unfortunately for Liverpool, he wasn't wrong. United became a tour de force in the 1990s. Ferguson, a spiky and forthright Scot, had developed a winning formula with a mix of skill, character, youth and identity that the people of Manchester could resonate with. Armstrong says:

> Ferguson tapped into what Manchester needed. He tapped into organisational culture and leadership. He knew full well what he was doing. It's really important to a football fan, particularly from the North West, that a manager has the same character and identity you want them to have. Manchester is gritty, it's in your face and likes to piss people off. You can see how Ferguson mirrored that. He really did tap into the identity of what an average Mancunian wanted to be seen as.

At that time, Manchester was a location also fast becoming a musical flagship for its decade. It followed on from New Order and The Smiths in the 1980s with The Stone Roses and Oasis in the 1990s. There was also a synonymous nightclub scene embodied by The Haçienda, a Shangri-La to the acid house and rave sounds that epitomised its era. As Liverpool knows only too well, music and football can often set the soundtrack and backdrop for a place and moment in time. In United and Ferguson, Armstrong felt the city now had both:

> From the mid-80s onwards, United were always a 'cool club' to be part of, if you like. The city felt the same and I always felt United was a huge part of that. It creates a feelgood factor that spreads into other aspects of everyday life. Manchester had just had a musical explosion. Everywhere you went [in the city] from the back end of the 1980s, everyone was just completely buzzing.

Liverpool had no shortage of defining character in the 1990s. Musically it wasn't standing still – especially on the club scene

Jürgen Klopp parades the Champions League trophy through the streets of Liverpool following the club's 2019 victory in Madrid against Tottenham.

Klopp and his trusted coaches Pep Lijnders, Vitor Matos and Peter Krawietz plot Liverpool's resurgence ahead of the 2023/24 season.

Liverpool's new manager takes in his new home during his unveiling on 9 October 2015.

Even the loss of the 2018 Champions League Final against Real Madrid couldn't stop the feeling of anticipation among Liverpool supporters.

Homebaked continues to act as a pillar of support and opportunity for the community in Anfield.

Amid a disappointing season, Liverpool and Klopp recorded one of the most unimaginable scorelines in football history.

Klopp announces his departure at the end of the 2023/24 season at a press conference in the company of CEO Billy Hogan.

The Premier League trophy is finally in Liverpool's cabinet.

The manager celebrates with supporters following the 2022 FA Cup semi-final win over Manchester City at Wembley; a day supporters serenaded him for hours with a tribute to The Beatles' 'I Feel Fine'.

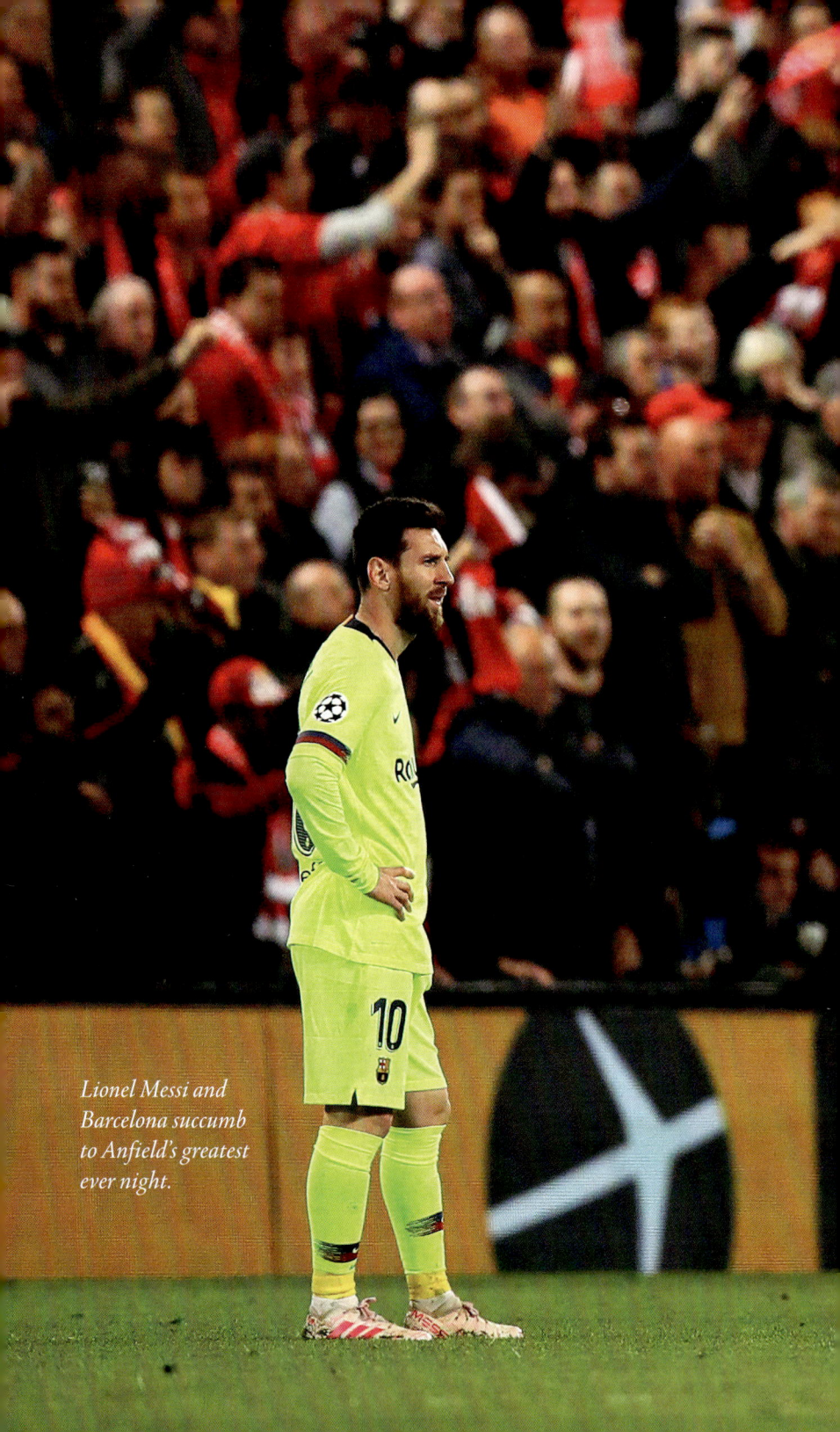

Lionel Messi and Barcelona succumb to Anfield's greatest ever night.

Celebrating victory against Newcastle United at Anfield on 1 January 2024.

The iconic Liverpool waterfront.

The latest Jürgen Klopp mural is unveiled on Randolph Street, a short walk from Anfield Stadium.

with venues such as The State, Club 051 and Cream playing the newest house sounds every week to the joy of revellers (many of whom were now partying to the effects of the MDMA explosion across the country). The city would prove to be a key player in the import of those drugs, thanks to the empire created by Curtis Warren, a Toxteth dealer with direct links to some of the world's most notable drug cartels.

Politically, the city would see hope turn to reality in the late 1990s with the landslide general election victory for Tony Blair and Gordon Brown's New Labour government and a planned, long-overdue regeneration of the city centre. If Liverpool was falling behind anywhere, it was at Anfield.

Roy Evans's Liverpool were entertaining to watch. They could be controlled but also cavalier; soon into his reign, stories of squad indiscipline would emerge. That narrative is now forever tied to images of cream Giorgio Armani suits on the day of the 1996 FA Cup Final, which they lost 1-0 to United thanks to a late Eric Cantona goal. The entire squad presented themselves in the oversized pant and blazer combo, complete with lollipop tie, looking sheepish and uncomfortable in the process – like kids on communion day walking past their mates in the park. 'We thought they looked like fucking nobs,' United defender David May later said.

If hero worship is something that has epitomised Liverpool since the days of Shankly, it was sorely missing in this decade. Evans was a well-respected figure, but questions always persisted about his ability to sit comfortably in the big chair. Across the M62, United were developing no shortage of figures their supporters would come to idolise. 'Hero status is underpinned by success. It's something which gets earned,' says Armstrong. 'But there's also someone else, like Cantona, who was aloof, a bit arrogant and in your face, with two fingers up to everyone. He represented something. The cities play a big part in that.'

Fowler, nicknamed 'God' by the Kop, was seen as someone who offered a different form of heroism through his renegade nature. He combined a truly stunning aesthetic of scoring goals with displaying support for Liverpool's dockers. When the 3pm blackout used to mean just that, it was his name you would look for when refreshing Teletext at home to keep tabs on the latest scores. But he alone wasn't enough to take Liverpool to where United were. From its inception in 1992/93, Ferguson won 13 Premier League titles. For Liverpool fans, what was worse in those early years was what he'd harnessed through a sense of identity and togetherness.

Many felt Houllier and Benítez could provide that for Liverpool, and in some ways they did. In both managerial eras, fans sensed a prolonged glory was at some point inevitable. Both Reds managers were cautious in different ways; they wanted things done their way, and they seemed to approach this with very little compromise.

In Benítez's case, he was fighting a battle bigger than any manager in the modern era had to face, thanks to Hicks and Gillett's amateur-hour, almost catastrophic ownership. The Spaniard would come closest to taking a title from Ferguson's grasp, in 2008/09. A team spearheaded by Steven Gerrard and Fernando Torres, was supported by the industrious and well-drilled spine of Dirk Kuyt, Javier Mascherano, Jamie Carragher and Pepe Reina. Xabi Alonso, the aesthetically majestic Spanish midfielder, was enjoying a Liverpool swansong before heading to Real Madrid in a deal that would be indicative of Liverpool's mismanagement.

Benítez's Liverpool were tactically rigid to the point of frustration. Three goalless draws at home to Stoke City, Fulham and West Ham – all by the turn of December – exposed both a lack of firepower and a clear distrust in Robbie Keane (a player brought in to bolster Liverpool's front line when it was clear Benítez's priority was Villa midfielder Gareth Barry).

Over the season, internal and external frustrations would manifest themselves through Benítez press conferences. The first came in November 2007, when he repeated the phrase 'I am focused on training and coaching my team' 15 times in response to various questions in response to Hicks's apparent order to 'quit fussing' about the upcoming January transfer window and potential reinforcements to his squad.

The Spaniard would also directly take on Ferguson before a match with Stoke on 9 January 2008. In what later became known as 'The Rafa Rant' by sniggering tabloids, Benítez highlighted how Ferguson was able to vilify officials and control fixture narratives but not be held to account. Both Gerrard and Carragher later stated they didn't understand why the manager felt the need to make that particular point at that time.

Any notion this cost Liverpool the title should have been dispelled by their 4-1 win at Old Trafford later that campaign. It should also be noted that Ferguson made desperate attempts to discredit his counterpart. After a 2-0 win over Blackburn Rovers in 2009, Ferguson seemed to criticise Benítez's apparent contemptuous hand movements following an Alonso goal. According to the United manager, this was a dismissive indicator that he thought the match was won prematurely and showed huge disrespect to Rovers' manager Sam Allardyce.

Despite the situation becoming slightly strange and conspiratorial, the only real fact was that United won a league they deserved to, and they had more experience than Liverpool in high-pressure moments. Liverpool's astounding 4-4 draw at home to Arsenal at Anfield in the run-in was evidence of nerves not being held.

Alonso left the summer after and the team gradually began to disintegrate due to a combination of poor recruitment, ageing players and a raging civil war that was entrenched in Benítez's day-to-day working life.

There's no way to know how Klopp would have dealt with a similar situation, or whether he would have come to Liverpool at all in that state. It would also be fascinating to have seen his Liverpool square off against some of Ferguson's best United teams. What's impossible to deny is the respect the German had for his United counterpart, and that he used what Ferguson did to form part of his own blueprint for Liverpool success.

United's best team was arguably the one that played from 2007 to 2009: a potent front three of Wayne Rooney, Carlos Tevez and Cristiano Ronaldo. Behind them was an industrious trio in midfield, usually comprised of Michael Carrick, John O'Shea, Darren Fletcher, or, when fit, Owen Hargreaves. A defensive unit able to squeeze the pitch by pressing high and a solid goalkeeper with great distribution was the final element for a winning formula. Sound familiar?

Ferguson himself has recognised the German's achievement:

> He has done a really good job and revived Liverpool's enthusiasm. It can happen that big clubs lose it. For two decades, Liverpool changed managers without building their own identity. You can now well and truly sense that you have to count them in [winning major honours]. You can see Klopp's dedication on the sideline – I'm convinced his work in training is similar. He's a strong personality. That's absolutely vital at a big club.

But there's something else, too, a point Armstrong mentions:

> Walking around Liverpool, you see how happy one half of the city is. When you have a manager who delivers trophies while enhancing the character of the city, you can't help but feel its impact. Having that association with your football club, through representation and values of where you're from and where you were brought up, people respect that – even outside of winning trophies.
>
> Football sometimes makes your city a better place to be, and Klopp gets that. Liverpool's success, as well as United's, was achieved by staying true to

its character and true to things that matter to their communities. These managers need to know they're in a place where they *can* be the best at what they do. Everything about Liverpool as a city fits in with Klopp as a human being.

Klopp clearly had a grasp of what Liverpool had gone through and what it yearned for. He used his platform to reassure the Hillsborough families in their fight for justice: 'Whatever your experience, I hope you know that you have the support, love and solidarity of every single player and staff member at Liverpool. What you have gone through since April 15, 1989 is inexcusable and our admiration for all those who have fought for the truth and campaigned for justice could not be greater.'

What's clear is that Klopp understands the city and its trauma. In bringing what he believes to the fore, Klopp has undoubtedly found a way to manage the team and marshal the supporters. He does so in a manner that allows Liverpool to solidify its identity and make it successful again.

Kavanagh states:

> He's got a God-given gift of being boss at football coaching, coupled with enthusiasm and the need to work hard. In Germany he had a club going against the powerhouse of Bayern, but he had seen the romanticism in achieving success another way [with Dortmund]. He knows teams can only field 11 players and be allowed the same number of subs, so it becomes about desire and building a team better than the sum of its parts.
>
> You had Liverpool, this sleeping giant with a hugely passionate, hungry and yearning supporter base with a thirst for winning, especially with a title absent for so long. It had become a holy grail.

[There was a feeling of] if we don't win it with Klopp, when are we going to win it again? The silence was deafening from around the country when he came, because they knew it was a perfect match, that the planets had aligned. You get in taxis and Evertonians tell you they hate the fact they can't hate him.

Chapter 11

Tell the World

THE 2018/19 season had left Klopp and his staff under no illusions: perfection was required if they were to deliver an elusive league title in what was approaching the club's 30th year of domestic famine.

They opened the season with a 4-1 procession over Norwich City at Anfield on a Friday night. Mané only made the bench, and it was Origi who led the line on a balmy summer evening with supporters in buoyant mood.

A Super Cup win on penalties over Chelsea, with heroics from new stand-in Spanish veteran Adrián, further whet the appetite. It would be wins away at Southampton and Burnley in August followed by victories at Chelsea and Sheffield United in September that really started to sharpen the belief that supporters were watching a championship-winning team.

All roads led to Man City's visit to Anfield on 10 November. In the previous league match, Robertson and Mané snatched victory at Villa Park in the dying embers, to the devastation of the home crowd and the elation of the away section. Van Dijk nonchalantly told a filming camera in the tunnel: 'That's what we do.'

Anfield was riled with adrenaline on the Sunday afternoon of City's visit. Klopp's team had dropped only two points all season, thanks to a dubious goal given to Manchester United at Old Trafford. A repeat of the previous campaign's stalemate in this fixture looked massively unlikely. Guardiola's men started well and looked threatening. They wanted a penalty in the early exchanges for a handball by Alexander-Arnold. It wasn't given, and 22 seconds later Liverpool were in the ascendancy thanks to a Fabinho piledriver, his first for the club.

An array of switches of play from back to front led to Salah meeting Robertson's deep cross for a second, and Mané made it three after the break. City were done and looked as chinny as they ever have under the Spaniard. Once again, a familiar tale of Anfield landing the knockout blow had been told.

City's stuttering form wasn't confined to L4. Defeat to Norwich in the opening month was also in the company of a draw at home to Tottenham and defeat to Wolves. The absence of captain Vincent Kompany and majestic playmaker David Silva looked significant. Klopp was in a forthright mood post-match, stating: 'If you want to beat City, the best team in the world, you can't try to do what they do. We have to push through our way.'

Klopp wouldn't be drawn on the title, despite going nine points clear. His poker face was shared by the Anfield crowd. The previous year had told them that City were never out for the count and that you couldn't rest on a single point with them on the chase. Chants of 'and now you're gonna believe us, we're gonna win the league', were conspicuous by their absence. Liverpool had been pipped too many times. They'd been hurt before and badly. Nobody was ready to let go.

That changed on 19 January 2020, when the final whistle sounded at Anfield after a whirlwind 2-0 win against Man United. The victory was capped by Salah bearing down on goal through Alisson's springing goalmouth release. As the Egyptian whipped off his shirt and celebrated in front of an ecstatic Kop end, the colossal 30-year burden was starting to be lifted too. At full time, the chant of 'we're going to win the league' erupted around the famous old stadium.

'Of course, they're allowed to dream and sing, as long as they do their job in the moment when we play, all fine. We will not be part of that party yet,' Klopp said afterwards. To the supporters, there was now no going back on the belief that the league title drought was coming to an end. Liverpool were 16 points clear with a match in hand in the New Year.

Only an intervention way beyond their control would stop them, and it almost did. Liverpool returned to Premier League action on 21 June as part of Project Restart, the Premier League's answer to the Covid-19 pandemic that had devastated the world and brought every aspect of life to a standstill. The Reds were a staggering 25 points clear of City, having played one match more. This was a matter of 'when' not 'if' the title would be confirmed, but the question of 'if' had morphed into something else entirely and left its mark on everyone affiliated with the club.

From trolling fans on social media to the agendas of Premier League club executives, ludicrous calls to scrap the season based on 'integrity' issues threatened to derail the procession of Liverpool reaching their rightful place. What's worse is that self-interest stood in the way of potential progress. For once in its modern existence, elite football had been brought to a complete standstill. The idea for reform was a space open to those charged with making the game work for all. Klopp's mantra has always been that footballers should play less, not more. Football could have taken stock and made things better for its clubs, players and fans, but it didn't.

Liverpool's season restarted with a 0-0 draw at Goodison Park, followed by a 4-0 win over Crystal Palace on 24 June to move within two points of the title. They would have the opportunity to clinch it against City in their next fixture, if the Manchester club failed to win against Chelsea at Stamford Bridge the following night.

Klopp and his team gathered at the Formby Hall Hotel on the outskirts of Merseyside to watch the match unfold. Billions of supporters around the globe watched on too, in different time zones and states of lockdown, to witness what everyone hoped to be the moment.

One of those fans was Ben Chapman – also known as 'The Bone' for his trombone contribution to Australian band Winston Surfshirt. 'With the time difference between the UK and Australia it meant that I was watching Liverpool win the league sat on my couch on my own in my apartment,' he says. 'Manchester City losing to Chelsea and confirming Liverpool as title winners was at about 7.30 am. Liverpool's long-awaited trophy lift was around the same time.'

Chapman was in England for the Champions League last-16 tie with Atlético Madrid fixture at Anfield prior to lockdown. He called me after City's match at Chelsea had finished; he and I had become friends over time.

City started the match badly and barely improved. Christian Pulisic had put the home team in front in the 38th minute, only for Kevin De Bruyne to equalise in the 55th. With around a quarter of the match to go, Fernandinho thought he'd escaped a deliberate handball to deny a certain Chelsea goal, but he was sent off and Willian converted the subsequent penalty. Klopp and his players waited for the final whistle in delirious anticipation of what was all but confirmed: Liverpool were champions.

Klopp and his players danced drunkenly into the night. Outside the stadium and its surrounding streets, a blaze of red pyrotechnics and jubilation took hold. Shadows hung from fences and posts – a night of reckoning in its own way. Liverpool had done it. Kenny Dalglish, Graeme Souness and Jamie Carragher all enjoyed champagne from their homes. Klopp tried to join them but he was so overcome by winning the title for the people of Liverpool, delivering something they'd waited so desperately for, that he had to walk away from the camera, crying uncontrollably.

For fans vicariously celebrating from within the confines of their home, it was a stark reminder of how much this manager understood: 'I had no idea I would feel like this. It's such a big moment, I'm completely overwhelmed,' Klopp said, his voice trembling. His emotion was shared across the planet, including Chapman:

> I couldn't have been happier seeing the Reds finally win a title for the first time in my supporting life. I've been supporting Liverpool ever since I was given a personalised kit back in 1996, so it had been a long time coming. The club had come so close on a few occasions so seeing them claim the title so convincingly was extremely satisfying.
>
> It's a weird thing being a supporter of the club on the other side of the world and in a completely different time zone. My celebrations for the title win and trophy lift was a few messages with Liverpool-supporting friends before heading off to work.

The next day, there was a citywide will to continue the party, but the pandemic raised questions about whether there should have been any gatherings at all. Liverpool had been crowned champions, but the sense of restraint was inescapable. Many resisted the urge to celebrate in public, but an unofficial gathering of supporters took place on Liverpool's waterfront the next afternoon.

The pandemic was cruel on so many levels, none more so to the millions of people who died and the loved ones who couldn't be with them. There was also the isolation and deterioration of people's incomes, identity and their everyday existence. For many, the sense of unfairness at not being able to enjoy a moment they'd waited their entire lives for wasn't the most pressing sadness, but it was still valid.

For Neil Atkinson and others it was the sense of community that had held *The Anfield Wrap* together, before and during the pandemic, which would be tested most. I can agree. It's the platform that gave me a voice on football, separate to that of a general match-going supporter. I'd always loved to write, without knowing whether anyone would want to read. At its heart, *The Anfield Wrap* has not only provided supporters around the world with a chance to feel the story of Liverpool from the heart of the city, but it has also provided opportunities for the likes of me.

Like so many local businesses it had to be resilient and adaptive. What should have been a monumental celebration required patience, despite the sheer scale of the moment and its context. Atkinson said:

> During the pandemic, we had to think of what the community itself was going through. *The Anfield Wrap* is about sharing an experience. You fall back on the value of authenticity, and the truth of the moment was we were in our houses and separated from one another. To think about the night we were confirmed as champions, we were able to do a remote audio commentary of Chelsea versus Manchester City, so we take the community with us and they can opt in free of charge. In the moment they're confirmed as champions, we're the same as everyone listening and on board with their reality of the situation.
>
> The community liked and accepted that. The next day there was a mass congregation in Liverpool. There were some key members of our team who went to that and tweeted from it, and that really pissed some people off. The reason why is that this is a community who didn't come to Liverpool that day, despite them wanting a party, but being told there wouldn't be one. I can understand why they felt that way, it was because of community. I think we walked the path of bringing the community with us every step of the way, with that one exception.

The manager and team would have to wait until the evening of 22 June against Chelsea at Anfield – the penultimate match of the Premier League season – to get their hands on the elusive piece of silverware, the absence of which had haunted the club for three decades.

Klopp made the exception of talking about an achievement before a contest in his programme notes, reserving special praise for the Liverpool faithful: 'Our supporters too, although absent since the season restarted, remain the wind in our sails,' he said in his ever-quotable style. 'It has been their wait, their anguish, their dreams. I hope wherever in our city, region, the country, or the world they watch from, they realise it is they that make LFC the club with the biggest heart and the most joyful soul in world sport.'

Millions would again tune in from around the globe to witness a crowning moment, accompanied by a pulsating match in which Frank Lampard's team refused to become part of the procession. The 5-3 scoreline had everything, including a riled-up Lampard accusing Liverpool's bench of 'giving it the fucking big 'un', in a touchline squabble.

'I think the fact it was a night game, and a competitive, intense game as well really helped the occasion,' Neil Jones recalls. He was one of a limited number of matchday press present inside the stadium for what should have been Anfield's most celebratory event in decades:

> It was possibly one of the best lockdown games I witnessed, played with quality and a pleasing amount of needle. I'm not sure you'd have gotten that with a 3pm Saturday against Burnley or Southampton.
>
> I was very aware of the fact that so many friends and family members were missing out on a moment I'm sure they would have dreamt of and imagined so many times. There was a degree of guilt in that respect, but also a desire and a determination to do

as much as I could to bring the night to life for those who couldn't be there.

If the match delivered, Liverpool were determined their alternative celebration would too. An erected stage in the middle of the Kop was to be the scene for Henderson's now infamous shuffle. It felt legendary in that sense, but also somewhat melancholic – a sentiment that Jones echoed:

> As a journalist, it was a somewhat surreal sight, the music blaring, fireworks and strobe lights and ticker tape, but all in front of an empty stadium. I thought Liverpool as a club did a good job in the circumstances, and the players all seemed to enjoy themselves, but you couldn't avoid the feeling of 'imagine what this should have been like' as Jordan Henderson and the squad were on that stage in front of the Kop.

For Jones, a Scouser who emanates from the Bootle area, this was what hit home most:

> I remember leaving Anfield, probably just after midnight, and there wasn't a soul about. The media entrance was part of the red zone, so was fenced off. I think that, possibly, was when the strangeness of it all hit me. I should have been fighting my way through the happiest, drunkest and most vibrant crowds I'd ever seen, and I wasn't. I was walking to my car alone, a 30-year dream realised but an unavoidable feeling of 'this isn't how it was meant to be'. I picked a friend up on the way home. He'd been to the pub to watch the game. He'd had a drink and enjoyed himself. I hadn't, and I didn't. And I was one of the lucky ones.

But, somehow, the dissonance of the situation didn't detract from the unity of the fact. For the likes of Kavanagh, the biggest weight of all had been lifted and a manager some outside had written off as a cheerleader had delivered on his first press conference promise to win a title for the club. What's more, he'd done so brandishing a smile and enjoying the journey with trademark vigour.

> It was so wonderful and as good as I've ever seen before. But it was the interviews he did that night and seeing him sob uncontrollably about what it meant. Rafa [Benítez] got Liverpool, but he's not an extrovert. He made us incredibly hard to beat and hard-working. This manager leads in every way possible. He brings the crowd on to the pitch. The holy trinity of the manager, the team and the supporters in tandem can achieve wonders.

Klopp had relished the journey and taken a city and supporter base with him. He delivered just as he said he would. Nobody could have envisaged just how it happened, but the curse had finally been lifted.

On 29 June 2022, a week after becoming champions and with Liverpool in the grip of the coronavirus pandemic, Klopp took it upon himself to write an open letter in the *Liverpool Echo*. In it he promised celebration, displayed gratitude and pleaded for patience among the people of Liverpool as the wait for a return to normality continued. He also curated a line that possibly best describes his own ethos and just why Liverpool were now champions of England, something so painfully yearned for:

> I already knew and liked the German word 'solidarität' before I came to Liverpool and now I have learned that the English word is solidarity,

because I have heard it used by our supporters during the last few months. For me, it is the word more than any other that captures what Liverpool people are about.

Part 4
Alone

Chapter 12

An Extremely Shitty Situation

IN THE lowly depths of an empty press room in Leicester City's King Power Stadium on Saturday, 13 February 2021 Klopp sits looking at a laptop screen, sniffling and hunched forwards. His Liverpool team have just fallen apart, losing 3-1 to Brendan Rodgers's Leicester, despite the Foxes looking second best throughout. A calamitous collision between Alisson and recently recruited centre-back Ozan Kabak summed up Liverpool perfectly in the moment. On the back of three previous home defeats to Burnley, Man City and Brighton, the Reds were without confidence, luck and, most crucially, hope.

It would get worse before it got better, with bruising defeats to Everton and Fulham at Anfield to follow. For Klopp, this might well have been the tipping point, the moment where the question 'how did we get here?' hit him like a ton of bricks. His entire system and ethos with Liverpool had been ripped to pieces by injuries at centre-back. Football was an empty vessel in every sense, with the absence of supporters and his team's title defence over with three months of the season still to play.

While Klopp gave some justifications for the performance against Leicester, he was his usual upfront self when it came to mistakes and the lack of quality that ultimately led to the game falling apart. As the interview drew to a close, he stopped to ponder a question about closing the gap at the top: 'I don't think we can close that gap this year, to be honest. We have to win football games and big parts of our football was today again really, really good,' he said.

Klopp explained that Kabak was new to the team, adding that misunderstandings can happen in football, before admitting, ultimately, the fact that his team had to fight. The question of conceding the title returned with a vengeance – Klopp moved his hands close to his eyes, seemingly becoming emotional in response: 'Yes, I can't believe [the question], but yes.'

Neil Jones recalls the sombre nature of the time:

> You could see, as that season went on, that something changed. Of course, there were setbacks – Van Dijk's injury, Gomez's injury, the swift unravelling of the title defence in the New Year – and there were personal issues to contend with too, but it was more than that. There was a sadness, almost an emptiness. I think he wondered, like a lot of us did, how much longer this would go on, and how great his appetite was to live life in this way. It wasn't football, not really.
>
> I remember the rumours that he was going to resign after that defeat at Leicester. That sort of thing happens a lot in this city, but it was believable at that point. It felt like if he turned around and said he'd had enough, everyone would have understood, because we'd all had enough.

Klopp's troubles had been set in motion almost immediately after Liverpool closed the 2019/20 season with a 3-1 win at Newcastle on 26 June. His players were back in action in monsoon-like conditions as quickly as 22 August with a 3-0 win over VfB Stuttgart in Austria.

The condensed summer schedule was also hampered by several positive Covid-19 cases in the squad. Klopp is one of football's biggest advocates for pre-season, describing it as a 'trampoline' for a forthcoming campaign. For him it can springboard a team into action from the first whistle (if carried through correctly and with minimum disruption). Before anyone felt like they could blink, football was back for another season in front of an empty Anfield on 12 September 2021. On the first day of the new season, Liverpool hosted newly promoted Leeds United in a massively entertaining 4-3 win.

Football's governing bodies had scrambled for months to make an already crowded calendar even more jammed. Having delayed Euro 2020 by 12 months, combined with a World Cup scheduled in Qatar across November and December 2022, and a raft of commercial and TV commitments to uphold, it seemed that any form of common sense over the welfare of players and staff had been dismissed. Interestingly, the impassioned plea for integrity remained conspicuously absent long into a season where matches were often postponed due to large Covid outbreaks at clubs.

Liverpool seemed to have a handle on their season with wins in their first five matches. The Reds won comfortably at Stamford Bridge, with new signing Thiago Alcântara making his debut after a summer move from Bayern Munich. Another summer recruit, Diogo Jota from Wolves, was showing himself to have an adept goalscoring prowess to accompany a high-pressing style. He was on target in one of Anfield's greatest lost performances – a blistering 3-1 win over Arsenal, in which a post-match Klopp was as front-footed as his team after Roy Keane had suggested that Liverpool were sloppy in parts.

'I just wanted to hear it,' Klopp said. 'I'm not sure I heard it right, maybe he was speaking about another game … it cannot be this game, sorry! That is an incredible description of this game, that was absolutely exceptional. Nothing was sloppy, absolutely nothing,' he said defiantly.

The discombobulated nature of football without fans was hard to put into words. The banners left on the Kop seemed to silently flag the absence of the typical wall of sound. It could also be seen in the muted celebrations of players and, at times, the completely irrational scorelines that football threw up (namely, the 7-2 away defeat against Aston Villa). The champions were on the back foot from the outset following a dreadful mistake from Adrián, standing in for Alisson, who was sidelined with Covid. From then on Liverpool fell to pieces almost every time Villa attacked. It had the feel of a meaningless friendly, a match where nothing was really at stake. After watching a team that had fought so hard for every single point under Klopp, the entire experience felt alien.

The Reds would have the chance to put it right in the following match. At Goodison Park in October 2020, they started like every wounded champion should as Sadio Mané put them 1-0 up in a flash. Liverpool should have trebled their lead within the opening ten minutes. But they didn't.

After a second-phase attack following a corner, Van Dijk was left in a heap from an imbecilic lunge from Jordan Pickford into his standing leg. The Dutchman's season would be over from the resulting ACL tear. Liverpool would also lose Thiago for several months following a horrific challenge from Richarlison in the second half. A last-gasp winner from Henderson was ruled out by the newly installed VAR, despite it seeming to be marginally onside. The match ended 2-2, but Liverpool had lost so much more than an additional two points.

A few days later, approaching a Champions League tie with Ajax, Klopp was still resentful of Everton's unruly nature in the Merseyside derby: 'A few days ago something that should not have happened in a football game happened,' he said. Midfielder Gini Wijnaldum accused Everton of 'taking it way too far in the games we play against them', labelling Pickford's challenge on Van Dijk 'completely stupid' in the process. From that moment on things seemed to descend into a slow decline of centre-back chaos as Liverpool's season began to unravel at the seams. Less than two weeks later, Fabinho was deputising at centre-back prior to limping off against FC Midtjylland on 27 October 2022.

AN EXTREMELY SHITTY SITUATION

Liverpool travelled to Man City on 8 November 2020 and were well worth the 1-1 draw that played out; however, injury struck again as they lost Alexander-Arnold to a calf problem. The immediate international break should have offered Klopp some respite, but for news that emerged on a rainy midweek afternoon on 12 November. Joe Gomez had suffered a serious knee injury during training with England, which would also rule him out for the season. Liverpool were now stripped bare of centre-backs, with Jöel Matip another casualty in the midst of their injury-hit campaign. Miraculously, the Reds went into Christmas seven points clear at the top of the table following a 7-0 demolition of Crystal Palace on 19 December.

But following that, they could only manage frustrating home draws with West Bromwich Albion and Newcastle over the festive period, which seemed to completely sap their confidence. That set in motion a torrid run where they won only two of their next seven league matches and went out of the FA Cup to Man Utd. Scoring just eight goals since hitting seven at Palace, a rot had set in. Jota had started Liverpool life in sumptuous form but was injured in a nothing match away to Midtjylland. Thiago also hadn't been able to get any momentum following the aftermath of the derby.

Klopp and Liverpool did act, making the out-of-the-blue move for Ben Davies from Preston North End and bringing in Kabak to bolster numbers at centre-back. Previously, they were able to outscore opponents, but their attack was blunted, and they were losing matches to odd goals. This wasn't a coincidence.

The gegenpressing system that Liverpool have employed since around 2018 relies on defenders compressing the pitch by pushing high. The players constantly anticipate the need to recover with pace and counter-press opponents with a relentless pursuit of the ball in high areas. Just as Frank had laid out to Klopp years before, when the press works it should stop the opposition from running through the midfield or having time to pick out quality passes over the top.

Active gegenpressing requires understanding and full commitment from each player. None of Liverpool's fit centre-backs had the pace or anticipation of Van Dijk, Matip or Gomez, and Klopp couldn't instruct his team with full belief to compress the lines in the same way. Academy graduates Nat Phillips and Rhys Williams were in the fold at this time and starting matches regularly. They weren't expecting to have been in the position they were, nobody was. Understandably, without the tactical experience and pace, the back line dropped off and wasn't as proactive when in possession. That led to Liverpool's front three becoming more isolated; the ball never arrived for them quickly enough and therefore they became much easier to mark.

By the time Liverpool arrived at Leicester in February, City had dismantled them 4-1 at Anfield. It was a performance that suggested belief – something so vital to Klopp's modus operandi since he arrived at Anfield – was being questioned, purely on the part of an absence of personnel.

Off the pitch, supporters seemed helpless to spur on the team. They didn't get the chance to laud them as league champions, but this seemed to hurt more. The mantra of 'You'll Never Walk Alone' has occasionally been sung in defiance, grief and even desperate hope. Klopp has called it 'the most beautiful song in the world' for its bittersweet declaration of joy. 'Everybody feels it, everybody loves it. Everybody gets the message. In your darkest moments, you are not alone. I love that,' he said in an emotional club video released days after another league title was finally won.

It was a sombre rendition when Liverpool were 3-0 down at half-time in Istanbul during the 2005 Champions League Final. It was the heartbreaking and poignant soundtrack to Hillsborough, the Kop's final day as a standing terrace, and the symbol of togetherness as the players joined arm-in-arm following the miracle against Barcelona. There's little wonder that it became such a relatable anthem to the people of Liverpool.

The song's origins are entrenched in a fight against establishment rule and a society stacked against the most depraved. Its provenance can be dated back to a play called *Liliom* by Ferenc Molnár, a Hungarian playwright who moved to New York during the Second World War. He wrote and eventually sold his play – based on the life of a man resorted to breaking the law in order to support his family – to Richard Rodgers and Oscar Hammerstein II in 1945. Rodgers and Hammerstein composed a heartfelt musical piece to accompany their new Broadway production, which they renamed *Carousel*, and called the number 'You'll Never Walk Alone'. The song garnered universal acclaim and was covered by the likes of Elvis Presley, Frank Sinatra, Nina Simone and Aretha Franklin.

In 1963, while on tour in America at the same time as Liverpool Football Club, local band Gerry and the Pacemakers gave a live performance of their chart-topping hit on *The Ed Sullivan Show* in the presence of Bill Shankly. The ever-quotable Scot was so uplifted by the song that he apparently told Marsden, 'Gerry, my son. I have given you a football team and you have given us a song.'

While 'You'll Never Walk Alone' is a Liverpool tradition that coalesces fans, collective supporter application continues to be widely contested. There are dividing lines over what constitutes support of the club and the perceived (often unwritten) rules that apply to it. These issues are bound to arise in a vehicle that contains millions of supporters worldwide. That the collective can be what it is at Liverpool is a victory in itself. Yet it's still vital that one doesn't take responsibility for every individual who pledges allegiance to the same cause.

In general, Liverpool's collective behaviour is represented by a support that's knowledgeable, passionate and far-removed from snapshot fandom. Not everyone can have access to Anfield, and technology provides an opportunity for different forms of fandom and representation to emerge. But the values and identity of the club are always paramount. Fans will get behind a team in its worst moments, provided it gives everything it can. Anfield can stomach defeats, it can acknowledge excellent opposition and can still find ways to laugh at itself; but, without the people who make it what it is, it was unable to do any of these things during the pandemic.

When Klopp slumped in the Leicester press room, he likely did so with the recent loss of his mother, Elisabeth, at the forefront of his mind. Despite the reality that he couldn't travel home to attend her funeral, the manager insisted he wanted these matters to remain private. But Liverpool in mourning wants to hold you and show you it cares. After the Leicester defeat, a banner was pinned to the railings outside the Kop; it simply read: 'Jürgen Klopp YNWA'.

The players were also clearly hurting. A squad of winners, who had tasted success at the highest level, now faced an increasingly difficult task just to qualify for next season's Champions League. 'It's been a tough period for many reasons. We are champions and we will fight like champions, until the very end. We will not allow this season to be defined by the recent results we've had. That is my promise to all of you,' Salah tweeted the same day.

The city began to swirl with gathering rumours that Klopp would quit. The toll of the pandemic, the failing season and his own personal loss had seemingly depleted his almost limitless reserves of energy. Klopp leaving would have signified what many were feeling: that what we were seeing wasn't what we knew and loved. The game had become a vacuum and seemed completely devoid of its main characteristics. It wasn't about Liverpool suddenly losing their credentials as title contenders, it was the sensation that the foundation of everything the manager, the team and the supporters had achieved together was being ripped from beneath them.

AN EXTREMELY SHITTY SITUATION

A few days after the Leicester defeat in February, Liverpool headed into a Champions League last-16 tie with Red Bull Leipzig, to be hosted in Budapest due to Covid travel rules. The day before the fixture, Neil Jones and other journalists logged into their Zoom accounts to ask the manager questions, not knowing what to expect:

> Someone from Liverpool messaged me before [the press conference] and asked if I would be kind enough to ask a question about the banners of support which had been draped across the gates of the Kop. I did, and so did Paul Joyce of *The Times*. Klopp's reply was great. Nobody needed to worry, he said, he still had the energy and he was still up for the fight. I think that made a massive difference to everyone, hearing him say it publicly. It took a weight off, and I wonder if it had a similar effect on him, to realise that people were worrying about him and that they wanted him to know they were with him and behind him.
>
> I wouldn't say I noticed an immediate change at the time, but looking back it did feel like Leicester was rock bottom for 2020/21, and that everything, slowly, started to get a lot brighter after that.

It came as a relief to the entire supporter base. It gave Liverpool hope for the future that with Klopp still at the helm everyone would awaken from this nightmare together. There would be a long way to go, although a 2-0 win against Leipzig lifted the mood significantly.

But Liverpool went on to lose another three home matches (one of which handed Everton a first win at Anfield since 1999). Again, in a Merseyside derby, the Reds lost another centre-back – this time in the form of stand-in defender Henderson, who, incomprehensibly, had featured as part of the season's 18th different central-defensive partnership.

'We were dominant in most of the games [so that means] in decisive moments we made a mistake or something strange happened,' Klopp said in his post-match press conference. 'If we make a mistake, they 100 per cent score from it. We don't finish situations off. We cannot change the situation by playing bad, but in decisive moments we need to improve, that's clear.'

The derby defeat was followed by elimination from the Champions League over two legs to Real Madrid. The last thing Klopp needed was another avoidable headache on or off the pitch. He was about to get one, which the football world would rally against.

On 18 April 2021, as the world made incremental steps towards a reintegration of society following the easing of certain lockdown rules, football was hit with the news of an attempted formation of a European Super League. A dozen of Europe's top clubs, including England's 'Big Six' (Liverpool, Man Utd, Man City, Arsenal, Chelsea and Tottenham), all announced they'd signed up to the new venture.

The idea was a Super League model that would change the current structure of domestic and European football by stripping the Champions League of its most prized names and effectively creating a financial ecosystem of its own in which clubs could distribute TV, broadcasting and marketing rights without being at the mercy of governing bodies. To many studying the intricacies of FSG's ownership of Liverpool, it had come as no surprise that John W. Henry had thrown his name in the hat.

Oliver Connolly, who I worked with while writing for Liverpool.com in November 2020, had foreseen something similar on the cards following the scrapping of the Premier League's televised pay per view scheme, writing: 'The likes of Liverpool and Manchester United, FSG and the Glazers continue to push for some version of the European Super League – be it the European Premier League, an expanded Champions League, or some Frankenstein version of the two.'

AN EXTREMELY SHITTY SITUATION

Previously, in June 2020, Connolly was writing about a proposed expansion to FIFA's Club World Cup, which Liverpool won in Qatar in 2019 after their Champions League success the season before:

> Most of the information and conversation surrounding the expanded Club World Cup has been centred on FIFA's desire to grab a slice of the Champions League bonanza. It is the top authorities' bid to curtail the power of Europe's top club sides (or at the very least get their beaks wet at the hands of the power class). It is believed a big-deal Club World Cup could potentially stave off the seemingly inevitable Super League, which would rip control away from FIFA and UEFA.

If some had completely seen this coming, official bodies seemingly hadn't. UEFA, taking the threat seriously, gathered its leaders and drew up plans to block the breakaway by threatening to ban teams from domestic leagues and blocking players from competing for their national teams. The Premier League wrote to its 20 clubs after its board meeting on the Sunday, warning them that league rules bar clubs from joining outside competitions without approval. 'This venture cannot be launched without English clubs and we call upon any club contemplating associating themselves or joining this venture to walk away immediately before irreparable damage is done,' it said in a letter to the teams.

Within 24 hours, Klopp had to take his team to Leeds United at Elland Road, where he knew he would face the media and watching world. The Liverpool team coach was met with abuse, and the persistent echoes of a saxophonist playing ABBA's 'Money, Money, Money' drifted into the stands from outside the stadium, while a plane flew overhead bearing the message: 'Say no to Super League'.

Back at Anfield, black banners had been erected outside the stadium denouncing greed and claiming the 'death of LFC'. Local fan group, Spion Kop 1906 stated they would be removing their banners of support from the Kop. Inside the stadium where the match was taking place, Leeds warmed up in specially designed T-shirts bearing the message 'Earn It on the Pitch, Football Is for the Fans'. The T-shirts were also left in Liverpool's changing room in the hope they would wear them. Klopp, however, was not in a complimentary mood and clearly found them insulting.

'I saw there are warm-up shirts, which we will not wear. We cannot, but if someone thinks they have to remind us that we have to earn it to play in the Champions League, it's a joke. A real joke,' he said. 'And they put [the shirt] in our dressing room. If it was a Leeds idea, thank you very much. Nobody has to remind us. Maybe they should remind themselves,' he reflected.

After a fairly forgettable 1-1 draw, the focus was again shifted to Liverpool's involvement in the Super League. Klopp was the only manager having to field these questions as Liverpool were the only team in action in the immediate aftermath. He could have been forgiven for being more irate with his owners for their timing, as well as the concept itself, but instead he remained vigilant and defensive of his team and the club's wider values:

> I don't think it is right. They put them [T-shirts] in our dressing room, I don't think we deserved that. I don't like the way a lot of people are talking about Liverpool. This is a fantastic football club. In this specific moment we can't blame the team for that. I take the criticism for everything, but this we have nothing to do with. Now people write articles about what they should do with it. People are shouting at us. We have to be careful because we are people as

well. We have to be careful. I understand all the talk and I don't like it as well.

James Milner captained the team in Henderson's absence and played the full 90 minutes. He added to Klopp's feelings post-match:

> I can only give my personal opinion and I don't like it one bit and hopefully it doesn't happen. It [the current system] has worked well for a long time. What has made it special what we have done over the last few years is we have earned the right to win the Champions League and earned the right to win the Premier League. The product we have currently is very good. It is difficult. Coming into the game today Leeds fans were making their feelings shown. As players we don't really have a say, so it feels a bit unjust. All we can do is try and win football matches.

Within 24 hours the concept was all but dead in the water. A mass exodus of clubs, including Liverpool, withdrew their involvement and issued apologies for any offence caused. John W. Henry was no different, recording a video that he sent out to fans via the club stating that he would take all the responsibility for what he described as 'disruption':

> I hope you'll understand that even when we make mistakes, we're trying to work in your club's best interests. In this endeavour I've let you down. Again, I'm sorry, and I alone am responsible for the unnecessary negativity brought forward over the past couple of days. It's something I won't forget – and shows the power the fans have today and will rightly continue to have.

The Super League, seemingly, has since become as forgotten as the pandemic. This may be to the relief of Henry et al., but it served as a stark reminder of the fragility of the entire footballing enterprise. Worse still, it appeared to give rise to the false perception that bodies such as UEFA and FIFA are the saintly safety net for the game – its moral arbiters who always act in good faith.

A notable absentee from the Super League snafu were PSG, allegedly because of chairman Nasser Al-Khelaifi's ties with UEFA. Al-Khelaifi is also chairman of beIN Media Group and head of Qatar Sports Investments. He has been appointed as the new European Club Association (ECA) chairman, replacing Andrea Agnelli after the former Juventus chairman stepped down from the ECA to take on the chair role at the European Super League project.

There are examples of questionable morals and ethics at the top of football's governing structure. Man City's two-year Champions League ban being overturned by the Court of Arbitration for Sport in July 2020, due to some of their punishments from UEFA being 'time-barred', comes to mind. So, too, does the continued arms race for Premier League TV rights, which has been a driving frustration for Klopp, FSG and everyone at the club. In this context, Liverpool are a prized cash cow.

The club has felt repeatedly flogged by Sky and BT with no regard for their schedule and an uneven distribution of rights relating to other Premier League clubs. Many clubs have become increasingly resigned to the behaviour of others in relation to Financial Fair Play. They feel they run theirs responsibly and within the rules laid out, while other clubs are allowed to find ways to circumvent the structure of law without punishment.

Dramatic sanctions were back on the agenda for the 2023/24 season. Everton were given a landmark ten-point deduction by the Premier League in November 2023 (since reduced to six points on appeal). Meanwhile, Man City still with 115 charges hanging over their head led to cries of corruption from Goodison Park. But corruption on the part of whom? The most significant oversight of the Premier League, UEFA and FIFA is that the operating model of the system has created entities more powerful and financially flexible than themselves. Clubs can allegedly flaunt the rules with increasing awareness that their mega-financial muscle allows them to spin webs of litigation and legal challenges to impede the flow of justice and bury attention. Everton's greatest handicap is that they didn't have the resources and power to match the punishment.

Man City continue to boo the Champions League anthem for UEFA seemingly having the gall to call them out on their alleged financial misdemeanours. But the anthem is now also routinely booed at Anfield, after the deplorable management of the Paris final in 2022. Many Liverpool fans hold a lasting grudge against UEFA for putting them in such danger and then trying to shift the blame on to them. It showed they're far from actors of good faith, but the entire Super League experience allowed football's major governing bodies to don capes and proclaim hero status that the entire football world seemingly fell for hook, line and sinker.

Klopp had to remain vigilant in the face of yet another massive disruption to his and Liverpool's campaign. His players, on this occasion, had vocally expressed their discontent at the Super League, with most of the squad issuing a clear and defiant message on social media caption: 'We don't like it and we don't want it to happen. This is our collective position.' Internally, they never stopped believing the season was salvageable and the manager was now in somewhat familiar territory.

It's widely believed there were times during Klopp's final year at Dortmund that it was felt his players had fallen out of love with his methods. They didn't want to run as hard or couldn't be as intense. Dortmund had fallen foul to Bayern's poaching of their players and were unable to buy as savvily as when Klopp first arrived. This, coupled with heavy injuries and a disrupted pre-season, meant things fell apart badly in that last campaign in Germany. The manager will have been only too aware of any perceived similarity to 2014/15, but there were many reasons to suggest Liverpool's 2020/21 stuttering campaign was different.

After the Leeds result amid the whirlwind fiasco of the Super League, another frustrating draw followed, this time at home to Newcastle. But May was the beginning of a bloom – the Reds secured wins at home to Southampton and away to United, where they ran out 4-2 victors at Old Trafford. There was a sense that Thiago – who had been instrumental in both matches – was starting to exert his true influence, and the team was beginning to find its balance again. The form of Phillips and Williams, in particular, aided such hope.

Somehow Liverpool's season was on a knife edge. Given the season they'd had, the Reds were unexpectedly on the precipice of some success. The depths and despair of winter with its demoralising setbacks, the inability to defend such a formidable title procession, and the dissipation of an unbeaten home record that had spanned 68 league matches prior to Burnley's win in January had left many feeling 2020/21 was nothing but a blank washout. But green shoots, or old roots, were miraculously giving Liverpool something to sustain themselves on.

As they headed into a vital match away to West Bromwich Albion on a brisk Sunday afternoon, Klopp had his team fighting a different battle with the same objective: win at all costs. Failing to qualify for the Champions League, on the back of a season where revenue losses across football were monumental, would have been potentially devastating to Liverpool's long-term planning.

The Reds weren't operating on a window-to-window basis under Klopp. With Gordon and sporting director Michael Edwards, they'd formulated a future-focused strategy that worked smartly and sustainably rather than reacting with a quick-fix mentality for recruitment. A possible absence from the Champions League may have created long-drawn setbacks due to the nature of their recruitment strategy. These would have only been felt later down the line when the squad needed replenishing due to ages of players in key positions.

At The Hawthorns the match was tense and scrappy, and the home team opened the scoring early. Liverpool responded well and equalised through Salah, while Firmino hit the post. Through the lines, Mané was causing problems for a deep-lying West Brom as he continually probed from 18 yards out, but Liverpool couldn't find a breakthrough. The Baggies had a goal from a corner chalked off for offside. Liverpool were in need of another miracle. Rivals have branded them the 'Devil's Club' for their Faustian knack to find fortuitous luck in the most unbelievable of situations. But for a club whose currency seems to be destiny, there was nothing diabolical about what was about to happen next.

In stoppage time they won a corner. Alisson had already decided he was coming up for it. Oddly, he took up a position around six yards out and remained relatively unmarked. Alexander-Arnold's in-swinging delivery was met by the Brazilian's glancing head and the ball flew into the top corner. Bedlam ensued. Liverpool's players and bench erupted. Across Merseyside and beyond, people completely lost control in their euphoria, unable to comprehend what they'd just witnessed. The pent-up loneliness of pandemic isolation seemed to find its outlet in the sheer human joy Klopp's team had unleashed on Merseyside. In every sense the dark was starting to lift.

According to Neil Atkinson:

> It correlated with society. There began to be an end in sight. The let-off and general feeling in that moment was about getting somewhere. If you asked me to pick a date when I thought Covid was turning, it was when Alisson Becker headed the ball in the goal. The thing about that season is that Liverpool get out unscathed

by qualifying for the Champions League. Suddenly things are opening up again and you get the feeling 'we're going to be alright'.

The Reds' goalkeeper, overcome with emotion, pointed purposefully to the sky. He'd lost his father in unexpected circumstances only weeks earlier. Just like Klopp, he couldn't be with his family. Just like Klopp, an entire football club grieved with him. Liverpool had won. They had two more obstacles to overcome in order to secure Champions League football. Hopefully, they would be entertaining fans in full stadiums the following season.

Liverpool triumphed over Burnley with a 3-0 win at Turf Moor that Klopp described as a 'semi-final'. Their fate would be decided at Anfield against Crystal Palace, crucially in front of 10,000 fans – the largest number since they lost to Atlético Madrid at Anfield on 11 March 2020.

So much had passed. Most importantly, people had been lost to a cruel disease in a pandemic nobody had foreseen. It was something that felt universal in its strangeness and discomfort. Something that impacted everyone's life. Things were no more about football, but then this sport bookmarks the lives of the many invested. We set our own watches by where we were and what we were doing at any point in our club's history.

It was impossible not to think of the time past, being back inside a full Anfield. Of the unknown when the Atlético Madrid match took place, and whether it should have at all. After that time had passed and revisionism and knowledge were gained, rewinding to that rain-soaked evening in 2020 reaffirms the sense of uncertainty it carried. That night at Anfield carried an unusual and discomforting feeling. The UK was behind the curve of Covid infections, but on the same course as countries such as Italy and Spain. At the time it felt ludicrous that the second leg of the encounter with Diego Simeone's team would take place under normal conditions.

In his pre-match press conference, Klopp became irritated by a Spanish reporter who had probed him with a condescending question around the responsibility of shaking hands, asking Klopp if he was afraid his players could become exposed. 'Are you from Madrid?' he posed, to which the reporter clarified he was from Argentina, but lived in Madrid. 'That's exactly the thing I don't like, that you sit there and ask me that question but fly from Madrid to here, so stay there. They close schools and universities [due to Covid] and you are obviously concerned but you think now football is worth [travelling for]. That's our common problem and we can't sort it with football.'

At the match itself, he was equally as spiky: 'Put your fucking hands away,' he barked at supporters who were hoping to touch players coming out of the tunnel. The city shared a similar confusion to the manager. Why was it that 3,000 travelling supporters from the Spanish capital had been allowed to travel to Liverpool to watch the match without any safety measures in place? A report conducted later in May by Professor Tim Spector, from King's College London, claimed that the two events held in March had 'caused increased suffering and death that wouldn't otherwise have occurred'. This was despite repeated insistence from the UK government that the Spanish fans had no impact on case numbers.

The intervening time felt like both an eternity and a fleeting trauma. The idea that 10,000 fans could be in Anfield to create a raucous atmosphere and drive them to one final push was an outcome that many doubted could even happen. But the supporters present at the Palace match ensured they made Anfield feel as full as they could. For the likes of Holden, it was a new page – the chance to go on another journey with this manager and his team: something nobody would ever again take for granted.

He and others roared Liverpool on to a 3-0 win from the Kop to seal European football and thank the team for an extraordinary finish in the most testing of seasons. 'Returning to stadiums was perhaps the most emotional I have been during my time going to the match,' he revealed. 'Palace felt like the perfect appetiser for getting everyone back in [the stadium] together for the new season. All summer I just wanted the new season to start.'

    Liverpool were battered and bruised. An everlasting image of Williams and Phillips bearing the battle scars of their endeavours came to signify the campaign in so many ways. The Reds waved goodbye to Wijnaldum, who had decided to join PSG. All around, there was the sense of one chapter ending and another one waiting to be written. Liverpool had found a golden sky at the end of the storm. A song about overcoming adversity was once again glowing with relevance for the club who adopted it all those years ago.

Chapter 13

Pie in the L4 Sky

BY DECEMBER 2020, 64,900 residents within the city of Liverpool had been placed on the government's furlough scheme to help subsidise lost wages as a result of government-imposed lockdowns in the UK. Thursday evenings out gave way to the clang of pans from home windows in support of the NHS. People had lost so much more than football, despite Liverpool being on the brink of domestic glory. The situation was the epitome of helplessness in a city known to help.

By mid-April 2020, Liverpool's hospital trusts were registering 51 cases of Covid-19 per day, resulting in a shocking 19 daily deaths. The clap for carers venture was a sign of solidarity but did little for NHS workers overwhelmed and unable to save those who succumbed to a cruel virus, and the woefully unprepared government who oversaw the reaction to it. A criminal lack of personal protective equipment and oxygen supplies meant that opportunities to stay ahead of curves continued to be missed.

By the end of 2020, 28,933 cases, 4,055 hospitalisations and 988 deaths had been recorded in the Merseyside region. The figures represented six per cent of the population of the region testing positive for the virus and three per cent of that number dying. The likely reason was that 92 per cent of those who died had at least one other health condition attached.

The city was in total flux. In the summer of 2020, Chancellor of the Exchequer Rishi Sunak launched the 'Eat Out to Help Out' scheme designed to provide a quick-hit boost to the economy. Restrictions were not only eased, but people were actively encouraged to go out and engage in a social activity despite the lack of any vaccination programme, or even clear projections on the future of the virus and its capacity to evolve and mutate. Just like Atlético Madrid and Cheltenham, the impact was clear.

In October 2020, Thiemo Fetzer, an economist at the University of Warwick, stated: 'The empirical estimates suggest that the scheme may be responsible for around 8 to 17 per cent of all new detected Covid-19 clusters (at least two new infections in the same area) emerging during August and into early September in the UK.'

Another lockdown was inevitable and imposed nationally early in November 2020. Figures from a month before showed that the second wave had resulted in 42 daily hospitalisations and nine daily deaths. Between November 2020 and September 2021, 1,683 businesses permanently closed. These would have likely included many local, independent and family-run shops in villages and towns that urban Liverpool communities had come to rely on.

To the surprise of many, in November 2020 Liverpool was lifted out of Covid restriction Tier 3 (very high alert) and placed into Tier 2 (high alert). People in the city were suddenly able to meet outside with six other people not from their household, and hospitality venues could open on a table-service basis until 11pm. Although city cases had come down two thirds since the second spike – much quicker than in other parts of the country – for many, it felt irresponsible and unfair that Liverpool was opening when other parts of the country weren't.

The Christmas opening helped hospitality and business in the city when it desperately needed it. But, as expected, people from around the country quickly flocked to the North West in a bid to enjoy some social freedoms. Before anyone could fully welcome in the New Year, cases had soared and another full lockdown was imposed on the country and city region.

A pandemic hitting in a city such as Liverpool takes on extra significance. The city had been plunged into austerity for over a decade previous and was already exacerbated at local level. Liam Thorp, the political editor at the *Liverpool Echo*, reported in October 2021 that Liverpool had lost £456m of its government funding since 2010. Incidentally, this was the year the Conservative Party seized power from Labour with a general election victory, heading up a coalition with Nick Clegg's Liberal Democrats. Thorp stated:

> The fragility of jobs lower down the pay sectors would be brutally exposed when the COVID-19 pandemic arrived. Liverpool went into lockdown, it was businesses in vital sectors that suffered the most. Pubs, bars, and restaurants were closed overnight. Music venues and theatres shut down – some would never reopen. The tourists Liverpool relied upon so heavily were not allowed to travel here. More than 31,000 jobs were lost within the city's visitor economy.

But the pandemic also exposed the greater health risks to those in the city as a result of generational deprivation and gaps in health and welfare. Thorp continued:

> As well as suffering the disproportionate economic impact of the pandemic, Liverpool's people suffered more greatly too. The city often found itself at the top of the infection charts and more people who got ill with COVID here would sadly go on to die compared with other areas. Much of this is to do with existing issues around health and deprivation. Research by the New Policy Institute found that the virus travelled more easily around overcrowded neighbourhoods. Almost one in seven, or 15%, of Liverpool's homes are overcrowded.

In terms of existing health issues, the city has one of the highest mortality rates for lung cancer in England and in 2018 it was estimated that over 6,000 people were living with undiagnosed COPD. These types of conditions made people much more vulnerable to the worst ravages of the virus, onward.

Before the coalition government came to power, local councils were funded largely through a system of central grant funding, which was allocated based on need. So Liverpool's major challenges in terms of deprivation were recognised via that previous formula.

When the coalition government began its austerity agenda, its eyes quickly became trained on local government budgets, and the process of huge cuts to those crucial grants began. Statistics from the Unison union show that in the decade from 2010 to 2020, grant funding for councils in England was reduced by a difficult-to-comprehend £16 billion. In Liverpool, £450m has been cut back in that period, roughly 65% of all the council's funding. A Centre for Cities report showed that a deprived city like Liverpool has lost around £816 for each resident every year.

The slashing of these grants left a huge hole for councils in terms of the support and services they could afford to offer. In their place, rises in council tax by local authorities were granted from central government. This system saw cities such as Liverpool, with higher needs, able to raise less from council tax because of the large proportion of lower-valued housing than in other, more affluent areas. As Thorp highlighted, this was felt most in lifeline support services:

> The government also encouraged councils to become more entrepreneurial in order to raise their own

money. This saw town halls trying to fill funding black holes by investing in businesses and property in order to try and raise more cash through business rates. This was never supposed to be the role of local authorities and you can see examples across the country of where it has gone badly wrong – nowhere more so than in Liverpool.

Being hamstrung by central government meant Liverpool required strong local leadership with the vision and integrity to lead it forward. In December 2020, Mayor Joe Anderson was arrested as part of a long-running probe into building and development contracts in Liverpool. Anderson was arrested along with four others as part of Merseyside Police's Operation Aloft. Anderson was also questioned as part of an investigation into alleged financial impropriety centred around Lancashire Council's BT joint-venture 'One Connect': the sister operation of the now defunct Liverpool Direct BT deal.

Liverpool Council's chief executive, Ged Fitzgerald, was arrested in connection with the probe in 2017. A court ruling in the case was told that 'Operation Sheridan had widened to include alleged criminality within Liverpool City Council and the Merseyside Pension Fund'. Anderson and Fitzgerald were told in April 2022 that they were no longer under investigation into Operation Sheridan; however, the former mayor – who stepped down in light of his arrest – remains under police investigation for Operation Aloft.

At a time when Liverpool needed stability, the very fabric of the city's local governance was fraying, with allegations of bribery and corruption. In every sense, a pandemic was the last thing the Liverpool City Region needed.

As the country navigated its way through the bleak winter periods of isolation and uncertainty, the prospect of mass vaccination offered hope of a potential return to an integrated society in summer 2021. The programme was rolled out on the back of approved trials by manufacturers Pfizer and AstraZeneca. As the country geared up for a cautious lifting of lockdown rules, not everyone was willing to roll their sleeves up for the jab. By December 2021, Liverpool had less than 50 per cent of residents vaccinated in some wards, and around 30 per cent yet to receive a single jab, according to government figures. Klopp, for his part, was effusive and openly vocal on the matter when asked around this time, telling the club's official website:

> My message around this has always been simple and clear, I hope: I trust experts. I follow the advice of smart, educated people who know their field because they've dedicated their lives to it and have studied it. I have no issue telling you I received my booster jab as soon as I was eligible and again that will be the case for many if not nearly all within our ranks in the coming days and weeks.

The manager went further and stated that a vaccination status of a player would potentially impact Liverpool's ability to sign them. Whether he intended it or not, he raised the attention of those who would ordinarily choose to ignore his non-football musings by bringing it into a sphere such as transfer strategy.

Klopp used his platform to reinforce the notion that he did not exist in a bubble away from others when it came to wider societal issues, just as he'd done on the cusp of the pandemic with the Madrid reporter:

> The 'stick to football' abuse so misses the point. Yes, I know about football, having spent my entire life in the game. And my view on the vaccination isn't from my own imagination. That's the point – I listen to experts. People who are smarter than I ever could be have come to the rescue of society by creating this for the world. We are very blessed in this country and

throughout Europe to have such incredible access to it. I see that as a privilege and one I will always be grateful for.

Klopp's stance was clear, but it should still be noted for its boldness and conviction. According to Atkinson:

> In the public eye, we got to see his emphatic support of the science at all stages. It's a reminder of who he is. I've often described him as a bit of a geek. Some people don't like [Klopp being outspoken on vaccines], but it tells you something about how he trusts those around him who know what they're talking about.
>
> He was genuinely desperate to get his message out and tell people to get the vaccine. He signposted people to the head of Public Health Liverpool because Klopp believes that's someone who knows what he's talking about. It was one of the rare times when he spoke as an actor – a public figure – to tell you how he views institutional knowledge.

MacCambridge agrees that Klopp's stance displayed the qualities he has that set him apart from his peers: 'Covid was a great example of how he wasn't just a good coach but somebody who had a sense of the larger world and a sense of empathy, not just for his players but the people spending money, time and emotional energy to get to Anfield, or for fans like us to get up at 6am to watch a game.'

As the pandemic persisted, the city's financial wounds were becoming deeper. At the time of writing, Liverpool has a quarterly economic income rate of around £2.1bn from retail, hospitality, business, motoring and health. Tracked performance of the city's economy showed spending drop below £1.6bn and £1.75bn in lockdowns two and three. The football club is pivotal to that in every sense. Liverpool FC positively impacts every aspect of cultural income and this has only increased, given the allure and romanticism of Klopp's tenure. It's a city used to welcoming visitors far and wide.

'Liverpool is a port city,' Rotheram states, and continues:

> It has looked beyond its own shores for centuries. Visitors are not only welcomed, but many of them also choose to stay and lay down roots for future generations. Fans from all over Europe come here to soak up the atmosphere week in, week out. In fact, we know that while 97 per cent of supporters travelling in from outside the region were coming specifically for the match, more than a quarter of them are likely to return to visit the region itself and would recommend others to do likewise. Supporters come to the city for football, but they return for our culture, and our warm, diverse and welcoming community.

At club level, Liverpool were said to be one of the lesser financially impacted. According to research from business analyst Vysyble, the club ranked seventh best in terms of mitigating their economic losses through the pandemic, The Reds' total economic loss was reported at £112m, as they lost out on £71.56m in 2019/20 and £40.43m in 2020/21. To add some context, Everton were last in the table with economic losses of £286.9m over the two years, with Spurs, Man City, Chelsea, Arsenal and Man United making up 16th to 12th, respectively.

Many put this down to FSG's frugality and their unwillingness to spend beyond what they deem as the club's means. Henry would likely argue this was Fenway delivering on their promise not to be reckless with an institution such as Liverpool. He can also argue that it worked. The club now seems in a much healthier and prosperous position than most others. Detractors will point to this being the Boston-based billionaire's Trojan horse that simply masks the fact they don't back Liverpool in the way they should. Of all football's oxymorons, attitudes to lavish transfers and the surrounding immiseration of the streets is perhaps the most difficult example of cognitive dissonance to accept.

For years, Liverpool have had to endure the tedious waving of notes from opposing fans to signify apparent class shaming. In recent seasons, chants around unemployment and poverty have matched the volume of victim taunts (chants from Leicester and Middlesbrough fans are often sadly ironic, as they're both places mired in their own deprivation and struggle). Although far less appalling, there are some behaviours that Liverpool fans are not exempt from when it comes to money in football. Many supporters, especially online, thought nothing of demanding the club pay Jude Bellingham a rumoured £400,000 per week in the summer of 2023 or splash out £115m on Brighton midfielder Moisés Caicedo.

All the while, the club remains at the epicentre of an area in desperate need of recovery. A 2012 study conducted by the Church Urban Fund claimed that Anfield was the third-poorest district in England. Despite its draw as the pilgrimage site of one of the greatest institutions in the sporting world, there are clear signs of dereliction and lack of opportunity. Around the stadium, local businesses remain either temporarily or permanently closed. Many are reserved for matchday trade only. Transport links into the area's mazy streets of built-up terraces remain scant. Admittedly, a 'Soccerbus' service is in operation from the nearest train station, Sandhills, which is a couple of miles from the stadium up some steep inclines. But it's the same service (and possibly the same fleet of buses) that I remember taking when I started attending the stadium in the mid-1990s.

The infrastructure of the stadium continues to be developed, with the Anfield Road stand the latest to be given new facilities and extended seating to take capacity to over 60,000. With it will come global footfall stepping into a neighbourhood that continues to struggle in every aspect. There are, as ever, ways in which communities continue to lift each other up. Liverpool and Everton were pioneers in the Fans Supporting Foodbanks initiative launched by Dave Kelly and Ian Byrne, the latter going on to become MP for West Derby. The idea used Liverpool's matchday crowd to encourage food donations for those unable to cope with cost-of-living prices and feed themselves and their families. As the initiative grew, it was clear this was affecting everyday working people, often those also looking after some of the most vulnerable in society. Today the initiative is a nationwide concept that supports the growing need to help people get by. Sadly, demand for foodbanks is increasingly starting to outstrip supply.

Another community staple of Anfield is the Homebaked Bakery, which sits opposite the corner of the Kop and Sir Kenny Dalglish Stand, but is by no means overshadowed. From a local business it has become a behemoth and prides itself on the quality of its pies named after Liverpool managers, past and present. Built as a neighbourhood bakery in 1903 and encountering the ownership of two families, Mitchell's bakery had been due for demolition as part of a Housing Market Renewal Initiative designed to demolish residential and commercial properties, with 1,300 new homes intended to be built. In 2002, Anfield was viewed as a 'market failure' at government level and the plan for redevelopment was hoped to boost new life and opportunity. Many residents objected under the view it undermined a once thriving community.

The initiative was withdrawn by Cameron and Clegg's new coalition government in 2010. In 2011, after Mitchell's (known simply on matchdays as 'the pie shop') had closed, Homebaked emerged. It had developed out of its initial identity of '2up2down', a concept supported by the Liverpool Biennial and initiated by artist Jeanne van Heeswijk. The project sought community involvement and had a vision of handing back control over development and the future of the area. The bakery became the site for public discussion and planning sessions where people spoke about their vision for Anfield, outside the parameters of the football club. Local residents began to come by and enquire whether they could buy bread, which sparked a desire to reignite the bakery with a community-led mindset. Homebaked was born.

Today it represents everything good about Liverpool and Anfield. Just like foodbanks, it has coalesced a spirit of action as people congregate in the area and come together to do good. The community remains in need of wider help, but any realistic possibility of a meaningful pledge to level up the country remains absent. In December 2021, at a cabinet meeting, £6m was committed towards the completion of Anfield village, a local government regeneration project dragging on for almost two decades.

'The developments listed in the report will provide essential retail and community facilities improving choice and competition for consumers,' Mayor Joanne Anderson said when signing off on the report. 'The final residential proposals for Anfield village and comprehensive site will in turn meet identified social need for social housing and assisted living.'

One constant has been the Homebaked Community Land Trust, which delivers on handing back responsibility to local residents and helps to shape a future in which they can have a meaningful say. For Homebaked, the battle for equality and prosperity in Anfield was being fought long before a pandemic struck, as the chair of Homebaked Co-Operative, Sally-Anne Watkiss, told me:

> The bakery has three key objectives and has had them since it began. We provide good-quality food for the local community. Anfield is in what's known as a food desert, with the only access to food [coming through] supermarkets, which aren't easily accessible if you don't drive. The bakery has been a bakery for

> 100 years, and we stick to the tradition of baking bread every day while sticking to supermarket prices so it's affordable and good quality, along with everything else we sell.
>
> Our second aim is to provide good-quality jobs for local people. We now employ over 20 people, who came to us as volunteers first and have other caring responsibilities or were a long way from the job market. By volunteering, they found a safe environment to get back into work. We provide wraparound support that conventional employers don't. Everything is tailored to supporting people. Our third objective is to provide quality training and caring opportunities for people to develop through our programmes.

Homebaked has succeeded in all three of its goals, thriving in building community roots alongside its quality, affordable food. Angela McKay, Homebaked's operations manager, knows only too well how that inspires people locally and beyond:

> People across the country look to us and say, 'If they can do it, we can do it.' That's a lot of responsibility. If we went down, we'd take a lot of hope with us. We show you can own a successful business run by the community. You can do something in an area completely dominated by football and you can buck the trend.

Fears that Homebaked and other local community enterprises could cease were hugely exacerbated during the pandemic. McKay added:

> We could have furloughed [staff], but if we shut, we didn't know if we'd open again. It was down

to marketing campaigns and partnerships that we didn't. We're not out the woods yet, the economic crisis means costs have gone up. We're still worrying and trying to think about our strategy going forward.

Like many others, Homebaked had to be innovative, adaptable and incredibly responsible to stay afloat. That sentiment is echoed in Watkiss's experiences from the time:

> The pandemic proved how resilient we are and how deep our roots in the community are. We laugh now, but we pivoted our business model eight or nine times during [the pandemic].
>
> We had to sell off all of the pies and produce. While that was happening we worked with the Steve Morgan Foundation [former Liverpool shareholder and Wolves chairman] to ensure money went to our staff and to then provide foodbanks. We had a scheme with Asda staff to ensure we were provided their lunches.
>
> It's actually harder now than before the pandemic because there's less help for businesses. The support is much worse now than during the pandemic. We're constantly working to find different ways to keep our head above water. The thing we found about the pandemic was that we found if you stayed open, did things for the right reasons and supported the community, the community (and grant funders to a certain extent) supported you as well.
>
> We had roots with churches, schools and other organisations, which meant there was demand for what we were doing. We provided over 1,000 treat boxes to key workers during the pandemic. [These] all went to the invisible people who were keeping us

going such as district nurses, ambulance workers and call centre workers for emergency services.

For ventures such as Homebaked, the sense of being independent from the football club is both necessary and refreshing. It offers Anfield's community a sense of independence beyond matchdays. The hope of more business in the area for international visitors to the stadium makes sense, but for a community that has been through so much, the need to stimulate the local economy is paramount.

It's a far cry from what Anfield was. It's not easy to look beyond the hardships of L4, but it's still possible to see the old grandeur of the area's houses, pubs and picturesque Stanley Park, which was opened in 1870. Anfield was once *the* place to live for many aspiring homeowners across the board. Anfield was part of a few affluent districts enriched by the transatlantic slave trade until it was finally abolished in 1807, and the more comprehensive Slavery Abolition Act was passed in 1833. The wider area of Walton and L4 was populated by doctors, councillors and business owners. Today there is less clamour for single-occupancy Victorian houses, which drive up maintenance prices in an area already blighted by challenges.

In previous years, neighbouring Breck Road was a hub of market activity. It would form part of a weekend day out, with local produce, clothes and amenities. Residents have seen first-hand that while the area hasn't massively changed aesthetically, its socioeconomic fortunes have.

Liverpool Football Club remains the central point of Anfield's local economy. If the Reds don't play, the pints aren't poured and the pies don't sell. Homebaked are just one of many businesses who acknowledge that they're still at the behest of matchday revenue, despite plenty of excellent community work all year round. They know that without investment into the wider area, that's unlikely to drastically change, as McKay points out:

We've now expanded to St George's Hall – an iconic building. We might be a little bakery in Anfield that is underpinned by matchday revenue, but the model works and we're trying to change that by expanding into the city and remaining affordable. We can only [stay open] because we're a not-for-profit organisation.

Watkiss states further:

We're always reticent to go for grants because it feels like we're failing. But we must remember having volunteers and providing training costs us money. It's difficult, because we try to fill gaps for the community, but they end up with another retailer, which only serves matchday revenue. Our business model doesn't work because it has to be reliant on matchday trade. We don't have the footfall and there isn't a lot of money in the area. We'd love more [community concepts], but we need help from the powers that be.

When supporters returned, so did the boost to the local businesses that had pulled through. Despite the uncertainty around the virus and its handling, Liverpool desperately needed its doors to reopen and people from nearby and beyond to come back to its bars, hotels and stadiums.

Its importance was felt on a different scale. Football in this city – maybe all cities – remains a release valve for the working class. People need the world to turn on an axis they've created for themselves. The pandemic left so many in the city feeling hopeless and without a sense of fulfilment, value and purpose.

Reporting on politics, Thorp is well versed in witnessing these kinds of sentiment in the city:

The two Premier League clubs [Liverpool and Everton] are utterly essential when it comes to the city's visitor and hospitality economy. That continues to be its lifeblood and is rebuilding itself from the damage of the COVID lockdowns. Huge numbers of people pour into Liverpool every week to watch football and soak up the atmosphere. Liverpool FC in particular has a huge global base and the city's hotels, pubs and restaurants are often full.

Football can be a great leveller. If you are having a tough time in your life, at work, at home or wherever – you can put that to one side on a Saturday or Sunday as you meet with your mates and head to the match. I think a lot of people badly missed that vital routine here in Liverpool during the pandemic.

Klopp's impact on these factors may not be as directly felt as his ability to coach a football team, but a thriving squad creates a striving demand to witness them on home soil. Even beyond matchday action, Liverpool FC are a source of inspiration and intrigue across the world. If more people flock to the stadium for tours and more local, national and global cameras are pointed in and around the area, the interest could invite both literal and figurative investment.

But that fight remains secondary to the ongoing one being fought by the true pioneers of Anfield, a place those cameras may only see as the home of Liverpool Football Club. Anfield will continue to be propped up most by its local community. For Homebaked, Fans Supporting Foodbanks and all other inspirational concepts that have blossomed out of sheer desperation, the will to be self-sufficient and preserve a sense of itself will last long beyond the leadership of Klopp.

Rotheram says:

We know from a study done by Deloitte after the 2017/18 season that the club boosted the Liverpool City Region's economy by £497m GVA [Gross Value Added] that year, which is incredible. The return of regular European football and the success of Jürgen's squad creating a tightly packed game schedule wasn't only leading to success on the pitch, but off it too. The club supports thousands of full-time jobs, and the wider ripple effect it was having on our visitor economy was massive, especially towards our recovery post-Covid-19.

Whether you're a football fan or not, it's an undeniable fact that when our local teams succeed, the rest of our region does too. We need our clubs to be competing for European football, because it's a massive win for our local economy. But the impact of the club's activity goes much further than just financial success.

Through its charity, the LFC Foundation, the lives of many local people have been profoundly impacted in a positive way too. In many ways, it's impossible to quantify the true scale that the club's success has had on the region under Klopp's leadership. He has given us our mojo back.

Part 5

Evolution

Chapter 14

I Feel Fine

LIVERPOOL OPENED their 2021/22 Premier League season against Norwich City in front of a packed Carrow Road, a stadium they'd loved throughout the years as it offered no shortage of dazzling displays and a feast of goals.

Daniel Farke's Norwich had been depleted by Covid-19 infections in the build-up. In general, the mood of society and football was one of wait and see. Many predicted more cancelled fixtures, more disruption and maybe more lockdowns, depending on the reaction to society reopening.

Klopp and his team were focused on winning three points. Liverpool had injury issues of their own, with a midfield of Milner, Keïta and Oxlade-Chamberlain. But it was the return of Van Dijk to the back four, along with Matip, who became as overwhelming a presence as the Dutchman himself. Liverpool had spent the previous nine months mired in defensive frailty and imbalance. Suddenly, they once again had a base for the team to build from and comfortably ran out 3-0 winners at Norwich. A rejuvenated Liverpool followed it up with a 2-0 win over Burnley at Anfield – the first fully attended home match since the pandemic hit, with a festival of noise to match the occasion.

'Good afternoon and welcome back to Anfield for our Premier League game against Burnley,' Klopp said in his programme notes. 'You have no idea how good it feels to say that. Welcome back! And a full welcome. A full Anfield. With a full away support. Football is back and it's wonderful.'

The journey hunters were well and truly on another adventure. From August to October, Liverpool were amassing wins across all competitions. They navigated tough draws at home to both Chelsea and Manchester City – matches in which it felt they would have won with more match sharpness. The Reds then followed it up with a 5-0 trouncing of Watford on 16 October as Firmino took home the match ball.

After three draws and five wins, that lack of early sharpness certainly wasn't a factor when they arrived at Old Trafford on 24 October 2021 – a ground Klopp where had failed to record a league win at as the Reds' boss. His team dismantled a shambolic United, despairing in the nostalgia of former striker Ole Gunnar Solskjær's inept failings as manager. United looked horribly disjointed in every sense. Liverpool handed them defeat as if they were almost literally teaching them a lesson – the manner of the win (5-0) was like a representation of process and plan versus, well, a lack of exactly that. The result was the culmination of huge amounts of work: from Klopp and Lijnders, to Henderson and Milner, right through to Edwards and Gordon. The two clubs had once again passed each other on the staircase, just as in 1992.

After the match, Klopp was asked whether it was one of the greatest days of his career:

> Greatest days? I didn't think about it, yet. It's a good day, a really good day and I don't want to be disrespectful. I have no idea, but it's a big one. We know that. Obviously after the game I got told that never happened in the long history of LFC; this group always wanted to write their own little chapters for the big, big history book of this club. This one was a little one tonight, a little chapter. People will talk about it in the future, 100 per cent, because it will not happen very often if it happens again at all.

The fans at full time were left in a state of shock and delirium at what they'd just seen. The away end was quickly on hand with incessant, ironic renditions of 'Ole's at the wheel'. *The Anfield Wrap* posted a video from the stadium in which supporters gallantly proclaimed it was the best thing they've ever seen that didn't involve winning a trophy.

'You don't win 5-0 at Old Trafford, you just don't,' said the *Wrap*'s Gareth Roberts. 'Now a new generation has got a tonking of Manchester United to keep forever. Anyone who went today, do not throw that ticket stub away. Get it printed ten times over and have it as your bedsheet.'

The team navigated a tough Champions League group of Atlético Madrid, AC Milan and Porto with ease – winning in Milan, with the likes of Tyler Morton, Takumi Minamino, Nat Phillips and Divock Origi all starting. Klopp was using every tool at his disposal to find all manner of ways to win.

While his team had firmly eclipsed one team in Manchester, there was another who again lay claim to the grandiose, mythical perch Sir Alex Ferguson once claimed he'd knocked Liverpool from. City and Liverpool pushed each other in a way the Premier League hadn't seen before. United and Arsenal had rivalry built on being the best during Ferguson and Arsène Wenger's time in the early 2000s, but this was something else. Guardiola and Klopp had created a title race with no margin for error, where mid-90-point tallies were the bare minimum for champions-elect come the season's end. It was a pace both knew they had to maintain just to take it to the final day of the campaign. The matches between them were equally as high on quality.

After the euphoria of Old Trafford, Liverpool had drawn with Brighton at Anfield, and the mood was dampened by the unaffordable dropped points. The intensity and momentum were back, but so was the pressure cooker of a Man City title race. If not for Klopp, they would have spent the last few years sweeping everyone aside without any meaningful competition.

Liverpool won 4-1 at Goodison Park on 1 December, leaving them third in the Premier League table, one point behind City and two behind leaders Chelsea. Draws were breaking Liverpool's stride though, in addition to some niggling injuries to the likes of Firmino and Thiago. A promising start from Harvey Elliott was cruelly set back by a serious ankle injury at Leeds.

On 28 December, Liverpool lost to Leicester City, 1-0. Salah had missed a penalty, a raft of chances hadn't been converted, and the final ball was lacking. Five days later they drew 2-2 with Chelsea at Stamford Bridge despite going 2-0 up and looking comfortable. They were 11 points behind City with a match in hand by full time.

After a 3-0 win against Brentford on 11 January, Klopp gave an extra punch in his full-time celebrations to the Kop. His mood was as defiant in the press conference moments later. 'I think the people are with us, they want to enjoy the ride,' he said in a relaxed manner. 'They are ready to go for as much as we can. This is not the situation to talk about a title fight, obviously. We try to do our part [in the title race].'

The result set in motion a run of 12 consecutive wins in all competitions – one of which was a penalty shoot-out victory against Chelsea in the Carabao Cup Final. This was Liverpool's first domestic cup final since losing on penalties to Man City in Klopp's debut season. The supporters had an indifferent relationship with the newest version of Wembley Stadium. In the 1980s the old stadium was dubbed 'Anfield South' on account of Liverpool's success and the regularity of their visits. But a move away from its roots and the temporary hosting duties of Cardiff's Millennium Stadium had left a generation feeling no sense of affection for Wembley.

Cardiff will always be fondly remembered as a stadium which was good to Liverpool in every sense. Houllier's cavalier cup-winning team picked up one FA Cup, two League Cups and a Charity Shield there, while Benítez also added an FA

Cup in 2006. The 2001 FA Cup Final, when Wenger's Arsenal outplayed Liverpool and should have been out of sight, was won in typical Liverpool fashion with Michael Owen scoring twice in the dying stages in the searing Welsh heat. Far beyond the lifting of trophies, Cardiff had a character of its own– friendly pubs and welcoming patrons, sensible policing and a stadium that held sound magnificently. It spawned a thirst for routine visits from a club that prides itself on gathering cups in May.

Those domestic gatherings had been absent under Klopp, with many criticising him for not taking the competitions seriously. His attitude towards the domestic cup competitions has always been the same; he believes footballers play too many matches and cannot maintain the levels without heavy rotation. If the Premier League and Champions League are the priorities, it's the domestic cups where that rotation will be implemented most.

'The attitude didn't change, I always wanted to go to Wembley,' Klopp said ahead of an FA Cup quarter-final with Nottingham Forest. 'It just didn't happen. For the league games you can make changes and then for the FA Cup the players are available. You need a specific amount of senior players available [so] that you can bring in the young ones but if you have to play only with young ones then it's really tricky.'

What was clear was that he and Liverpool were challenging with the healthiest squad seen at the club in decades. Guardiola and City usually operated with 13 to 15 key players who were seemingly always in relative rude health. Chelsea could boast a squad of 18 good players, although not perhaps at the level of consistency shown by Liverpool and Man City. Klopp had amassed 22 to 25 excellent options for his squad across four competitions.

Miraculously, they all managed to remain focused and positive. Players such as Takumi Minamino – brought in January 2020 after a mesmerising performance for Red Bull Salzburg at Anfield in the Champions League – went on to net ten times, seven of which came in domestic cup competitions. The squad rightly prioritised players based on their worth to the team, but it was a testament to the club's everyday harmony that even those on the periphery were performing to such an elevated and dedicated level when called upon.

Klopp said, after the Japanese international moved to Monaco in the summer of 2022:

> I'm sure there will be those who think it didn't quite work out [at Liverpool]. Those who think this are wrong. I don't accept that. An amazing professional; super, talented player. As a person, he is full of warmth and makes everyone feel positive. A manager's dream, to be honest. His contribution far outweighs the opportunities we were able to give, in terms of starting matches. He made us better each and every day he was with us – perfect attitude, winner's mentality. His achievements here will stand the test of time.

Once again, this was a sign of what can be achieved with togetherness. Klopp had displayed this from almost the first minute of his Liverpool tenure. This was an entire city that had to learn, under horrendous circumstances, the true value of that quality. As the players stood arm-in-arm with the Carabao Cup on a cold February evening in the capital, there was a feeling something special could be achieved with this specific group at this specific moment.

If there was anticipation building in the stands, the focus was only sharpening in the Liverpool dressing room. Henderson was bullish about the fact Liverpool just needed to focus on the next match, straight after he'd lifted the Carabao Cup:

> At the start of the season, you never set out to go for certain trophies and not go for them. We'll take each

game, not matter what competition it is, take each game as it comes, go for every single game and it's worked okay so far. So hopefully we can just continue on that road and in the near future, hopefully there's more trophies to be won.

Following the cup win, Liverpool were straight back to work, finishing the job of going 2-0 up against Inter Milan to qualify for the Champions League quarter-final, despite losing 1-0 in the return leg. When they won 2-0 at Brighton on 12 March, they'd astonishingly moved ten points clear of Chelsea and within one of City, who could only manage a goalless draw with Crystal Palace at Selhurst Park. At one stage they'd been 14 points behind Guardiola's men, but they'd made up the distance admirably.

Wins against Arsenal, Watford, Nottingham Forest and Benfica took Liverpool to the Etihad Stadium in good shape. Against City, the game had its usual pulsating feel of a boxing match between two prime, prizefighters: each took their turn to pin the other against the ropes and let loose with a flurry of damaging blows. The scoreline, incredible on the eye, was in City's favour as they led 2-1 at half-time. Klopp and his team worked on showing Liverpool where better decision-making could have garnered better results. An early equaliser through Mané lifted the away team into the ascendancy, but they still couldn't find a winner.

'I don't know if Jürgen respects me but Jürgen has to know I respect him a lot,' Guardiola said post-match. 'He has made me a better manager. His team is always there, they are always aggressive. We are not friends, we never see each other, I have his number but I don't call him. I have respect for him, but he knows next Saturday [in the FA Cup semi-final] I am going to try and beat him.' Guardiola jokingly added to NBC Sport: 'They are so annoying, honestly.'

The annoying Reds would once again descend on Wembley Way for a place in the FA Cup Final, coming up again against a City team, in the middle of a bruising Champions League double-header with Diego Simeone's Atlético. For Liverpool supporters, the match would take care of itself. The hint of summer sun and the sound of a new beat to the tune of The Beatles' 'I Feel Fine' had London humming to the beat of anticipation and what the run-in could bring.

> Jürgen said to me, 'You know we'll win the Premier League,' you know, he said so. I'm in love with him and I feel fine. I'm so glad, that Jürgen is a Red. I'm so glad, he delivered what he said.

The song could be heard in pubs miles away from the ground. It was the pin in the map of a special place in time. Early goals from Konaté and Mané inspired the intensity and elation of the moment, as Liverpool ran all over City to go three goals up by half-time.

The concourses of Wembley shook with repeated verses of the chant and a sheer mesmerising disbelief of what this team and manager were achieving. City clawed two goals back, but Liverpool deservedly went through to set up another encounter with Chelsea and book a second date in the calendar for the stadium.

Victory over Benfica meant a Champions League semi-final with Villarreal. By April the team again outclassed Manchester United, winning 4-0 at Anfield with a first-half display full of aggression and superiority in every department. A 2-0 win over Everton, with Origi adding a customary goal against the neighbours, further boosted the feelgood nature of the momentum that was being built.

In their European campaign, the Reds led 2-0 after the first leg of the tie with Unai Emery's Villarreal at Anfield. The Spaniard, who has since gone on to manage Aston Villa to great acclaim, is renowned for his tactical nous, especially in knockout conditions. Emery would have a plan for Liverpool in the return leg, and went 2-0 up in the first half to leave Klopp and Liverpool shell-shocked. Klopp later said:

> They played pretty much very man-orientated, if not man-marking. In a lot of moments they took all the risk; I couldn't respect it more what they did. The physical aspect at least, we didn't mention at half-time. No, I cannot tell you what I said at half-time [because], first and foremost, I don't know it exactly anymore, but I know what I was talking about. About playing football and where we have to play, where we have to move, where we have to show up, where we have to be brave, where we have to change the momentum, where we have to go in behind and where we have to go in between.
>
> It was a football problem, and understanding football problems you sort with football if you can get your mind right. After three minutes, our mind was not right anymore – we were in a rush, we felt the pressure and that doesn't make sense. You have to force your own football through, and in the second half we did that.

That force was applied straight after the restart, and an early goal from Fabinho swung the tie back in Liverpool's favour. Strikes from exciting January arrival Luis Díaz, and then Mané booked the Reds a place in Paris for the final: Klopp's third as Liverpool manager. His team had made history as the first to reach the final of each of the Champions League, FA and Carabao Cup in one season. Liverpool were about to enter their 12th European final. For a domestic league often seen as the benchmark for quality, the scarce nature of European success only further exemplifies how Liverpool's standing as continental royalty had been reinforced beyond imagination by the German.

More pertinent was the possibility of an unprecedented quadruple. Klopp's team would head into the final day of the season a single point behind City. The team had secured dramatic 2-1 wins away to Aston Villa and Southampton either side of securing the FA Cup via another shoot-out win against Chelsea. On this Wembley trip, Kostas Tsimikas was the hero after only six penalties (compared to the 11 nailbiters back in March). The domestic double at Wembley was complete, but the following day headlines displayed outrage over Liverpool's loud and visceral booing of the national anthem and the introduction of Prince William.

'Anger As Liverpool Fans Boo William' ran the *Daily Mail* headline. Despite not being a comment piece, it quoted other outraged political figures to make its point. Among the highest in profile was Sir Lindsay Hoyle, speaker of the House of Commons, who denounced the act as 'shameful'. 'I utterly condemn any fans who booed Prince William at Wembley today. The FA Cup final should be an occasion when we come together as a country. It should not be ruined by a minority of fans' totally shameful behaviour. In this year of all years – the Queen's Platinum Jubilee – this is dreadful.'

Tory MP for Staffordshire and former Secretary of State for Northern Ireland Karen Bradly weighed in and urged the FA to 'pursue those responsible'. Quite where Hoyle, Bradly or *The Mail* had been for the Carabao Cup Final, or any Wembley showpiece attended by Liverpool since 1965 – when supporters resorted to a more playful chant of 'God Save Our Team' – is anyone's guess.

The booing of the national anthem shouldn't have come as a shock to anybody, since it had happened only three months prior without any meaningful comment. Yet the *Daily Mail* felt the need to pursue the story and seek out Liverpool fans on Twitter who didn't agree with the actions of their fellow fans. There was plenty of defence for William and some for the singer RAYE, who both may have thought the booing was especially reserved for them in particular. It wasn't. If this book has detailed anything about Liverpool's strife as a city, it's the feeling of being let down by the establishment that serves it.

The expression of displeasure was a response to crippling inequality and economic neglect, which has spanned decades. It serves as a vent for frustrations towards the government. It's a small act of rebellion against marginalisation. As the country feels the full force of a cost-of-living crisis – which has only been worsened by government action – those who aren't fighting for their next meal or are petrified about the next energy bill are shaking their liberal heads in disbelief, while for many in the city it's simply the case of everyday life. Initiatives started in the city, such as Fans Supporting Foodbanks, are an indication that things have been a certain way in Liverpool for a long time before now.

Hillsborough, Toxteth and Churchill's crusade of gunboats up the Mersey have left the city with a feeling of disassociation. Every city has its traits. The ability to fight together and stand up for itself are among Liverpool's best. But rebellion and distrust can also lead to paranoia and conspiracy.

In September 2023, former Reds striker Rickie Lambert attended protests outside Liverpool Town Hall. He was joined by other demonstrators wishing to voice their lack of consent towards the implementation of 15-minute cities, an urban planning concept designed to provide all necessary amenities within a 15-minute radius. The protest was accompanied with slogans such as 'Climate Change is a Hoax' and was roundly mocked.

The home and travelling Kop has continued its vociferous anti-Tory chanting as the country's plight has worsened in recent years. There are those who stand among those chants, disgruntled by the view that football and political views shouldn't mix (a criticism Klopp has faced on numerous occasions). Then there are also those who dedicate their entire lives to fighting political and establishment oppression and therefore don't have the energy to continue when it comes to their favourite leisure activity.

But to understand Liverpool is to understand more than a squad of players, its best XI and formation. The nuances and passion that give the club its emotional essence remain among its most identifiable features. Klopp, when asked about the booing after Liverpool's Community Shield win in July, stated:

> They wouldn't do if there was no reason. I've not been here long enough to understand the reason for it – it's for sure something historical – and that's probably questions you can answer much better than I could ever. The majority of our supporters are wonderful people. Really smart, go through lows and highs. They wouldn't do it without reason.

There was no time for anyone associated with the club to get distracted by headlines in the 2021/22 run-in. Anfield would soon be packed to the rafters on 22 May, providing Klopp with his second title-decider with City on the final day of a league campaign. The visitors? Wolverhampton Wanderers yet again, just as in 2018/19.

Many supporters entered feeling a sense of pride regardless of the outcome. City faced off against Steven Gerrard's Aston Villa at the Etihad in a match many expected to be a formality. Having lost out on a title win in identical circumstances to Guardiola's team in 2018/19, the hope that characteristic fate might intervene this time left a nervous energy in the air. This wasn't helped when an early misjudgement from Ibrahima Konaté allowed Wolves an opening, and the visitors were ahead within three minutes at Anfield.

Mané's equaliser on 24 minutes eased some tensions, but news that Villa had gone one up in Manchester began to spread around the stadium. Anfield erupted into a throng of mass delirium. It was elation matched with frustration; calm intermingled with chaos. Whatever happened elsewhere, Liverpool still just needed to look after their own fate. The permutations, timelines and anxieties were all out. It wasn't helping those on the pitch in red. For everyone there was a desire for Liverpool to be in full control of the situation; but the fact remained that if City won, they would take the title with them.

When Coutinho, of all people, put Villa two goals to the good across the M62, bedlam ensued. The crowd had almost forgotten that Liverpool needed to win to make anything possible. For six minutes Anfield was the most unhinged and frenzied it had been in its long history. Five minutes was all it took for City to completely turn the match on its head and gain the mastery they rarely relinquish. Goals from Salah and Robertson on 84 and 89 minutes were futile. History had indeed been repeated and Liverpool were pipped by a point, with 90-plus on the board in the final reckoning.

This felt like an extra blow given that prior to 2016/17 that particular point bracket had only been hit six times since the Premier League's formation in 1992. The Reds' 92 points would have been enough to win the league in most other seasons. 'Story of my life,' quipped Klopp. 'I'm still the record holder for not getting promoted in Germany from second to first division with the highest number of points. I have the second highest points tally as well but it's okay,' he said to Sky's Kelly Cates on the Anfield turf, as the players did their customary lap of the pitch.

Supporters were in a similar place of immediate disappointment, but this was somewhat eased by the prolonged sense of hope that came from the opportunity to win a seventh European Cup against Real Madrid. The Spanish team had wrapped up La Liga weeks before, while the Reds were walking wounded as they headed to Paris for the showpiece, with Thiago and Fabinho their major injury concerns. Liverpool had rotten luck against Madrid under Klopp. In each of the three defeats – the 2018 Champions League Final and both legs of the 2021 quarter-final – there were obvious caveats. The injury to Salah in Kyiv and the mass casualties of the season previous had left everyone feeling that, in the right circumstances, Liverpool could prevail over Carlo Ancelotti's team.

Madrid had hung in the competition by a thread, getting past Chelsea and City in extra time despite both ties seeming heavily stacked against them for large periods. They were dangerous operators who had the experience of players such as Luka Modrić, Toni Kroos and Karim Benzema, coupled with the youthful attacking flair of Vinícius Jr and Eduardo Camavinga. For all the talk of revenge in the air, Klopp seemed in a somewhat reflective mood in his media duties, saying in an interview with UEFA in the build-up to the final:

> I don't know what I want people to think about me. What I want to do for the club is set up a structure and a culture for now and after I leave because the right structure and the right culture should not depend on people; it should depend on the club. If things are right, then it's right, so keep using it in the future. So, that's it. That's my aim, really. Okay, I only have the time to do that if we win things on that path.
>
> People never ask me what kind of legacy I want to have at a football club, but I once got asked what I want to have on my gravestone. Honestly, it was like, 'He was a nice fella.' That would absolutely be enough because all the rest is ... That's actually my only real concern: that I don't have to knock other people down to be successful. It's never happened so far, so I won't start it now.

The line about not knocking others down to be successful has been aired before by the Liverpool manager, most notably in reference to his Christian faith. Klopp has cited that one of the few conflicts he faces as a football manager is that he likes to see others have success. In a 2016 interview with fr-online.de, he said openly:

> The problem is I'm a Christian. That [in itself] is not a problem, but the problem is I think other people can have success too – it's not about me. But if you ask me about Liverpool I would like to celebrate something each season. To be a believer, but not to want to talk about it – I do not know how it would work! If anyone asks me about my faith, I give information. Not because I have claim to be any sort of missionary. But when I look at me and my life – and I take time for that every day – then I feel I am in sensationally good hands.

Klopp's charismatic ability to use words affably, insightfully and transparently in whatever conversation he's engaged in remains one of his most impressive traits. Religion can be a divisive factor for communities, countries and entire continents, but the Liverpool manager uses his to be open and honest, to embrace journeys and people. It would be remiss of any supporter who has gone on the journey with him and the club since 2015 not to have gleaned at least something from his outlook. Football remains one of society's most tribal environments, often because of infighting between factions of a club's own fanbase.

Klopp often reiterates that he 'cannot help' those who seemingly only experience football as a means to criticise and judge solely on issues such as the transfer activity of their club. He has strived to teach a club to be positive in defeat so it can learn to become successful. In achieving just that, human qualities have undoubtedly filtered from Klopp into the city. In time, his legacy will mean much more than simply returning trophy success to one of the world's greatest clubs.

Some may argue his team should have won more. Three Champions League finals and one success to date. Two final-day title-deciders and none going in his favour. A team stacked with so much talent and an attitude that justified their 'mentality monsters' moniker. As the manager knows only too well, the difference between a rubber stamp of success and the loneliness of the silver medal comes down to the finest of margins.

By the time kick-off had been delayed for the second time in Paris, many supporters present had lost the volition to see Liverpool win on the pitch. The nightmare of Saint-Denis. The thousands trapped outside with genuine tickets and treated with utter contempt, exacerbated by the fear of uncertainty for what lay in store after the match. And the all too familiar emergence of a shifting of blame on to fans. Supporters were left numb.

On the pitch, reporters gave different accounts about the fitness of Thiago in the warm-up and there was some confusion about whether he would actually start. The match got underway with him on the pitch, but in truth the entire encounter felt somewhat hollow. Despite being the better team, Liverpool were thwarted time and again by Thibaut Courtois – the former Chelsea goalkeeper. Salah and Mané probed to no avail, and when Madrid got in down Liverpool's left early in the second half to take the lead through Vinícius, the sense of inevitability was pervasive.

The Reds had come within a whisker of becoming the first team in English football history to win all four trophies in one season. That statistic alone is perhaps key to why it didn't happen. To win four trophies requires an incredible amount of skill, desire and considerable luck. When so much is at stake, the margins become finer than gossamer – split seconds start the chain reactions that decide the outcome. Things need to go in your favour at key moments. It becomes a case of minutes and seconds rather than weeks and months. Villa's collapse and Courtois's career-defining evening meant the result shifted slightly the other way.

Unfortunately, for the thousands present and inside the stadium, the pre-match fears of policing and abject mismanagement were realised again after the whistle. Exits from the stadium were blocked off. Gates that should have been open were closed, leaving many climbing their way out or unable to find an exit. This was supposed to be (as if a reminder were needed) the showpiece event of the football calendar.

Outside, things were much worse. Local gangs and police seemed intent on causing further harm to petrified supporters. The fear for personal safety was paramount for men, women and children who had come to watch their team play football. 'The smallest problem after a game like this is that we lost the game,' said Klopp some weeks later. He argued:

> It says it all. It's why everyone, the authorities, have to make sure this does not happen again. It was clear where it was [held] was a problem. I think in Paris, the authorities would have known about the regional issues there. Anyway, UEFA decided pretty quick that it will be in Paris. There were other cities where it could have been held. I understand that they got the information pretty late [that it was the host venue]. There was not one Liverpool supporter in the wrong spot. There were a lot of spots occupied definitely by people without tickets, but they were not Liverpool supporters.

There was deflation and a sense of tiredness on and off the pitch. Liverpool had navigated their way through 63 fixtures over the course of one season. Most of the squad would have to join up with their international teams for pointless Nations League matches in the aftermath, delaying a well-earned summer holiday.

Before any of that, Liverpool had a commitment to keep. Klopp and the club had made the decision to parade through the city streets regardless of the outcome in Paris. This was in part a promise kept by the Liverpool manager following the Covid-19 outbreak and the inability to be together and celebrate the Premier League success. With two trophies already in the bag there was a feeling that this was a cause for celebration, no matter what.

But on a gloomy Merseyside morning on 29 May, there weren't many in the Liverpool squad who felt like celebrating. More still, there was a concern that nobody would show up, given the way the season had played out. Liverpool had failed in the most beautiful way possible, to quote Klopp's Barcelona team talk. The impact of the season would need time to settle on everyone.

From the moment the bus was in motion, the city was adorned in red; the players were cheered and welcomed along every stretch of its route through Queens Drive and into the city centre. As they turned into The Strand – just as they'd done in 2019 with the Champions League trophy – a look of disbelief washed over the players. The sea of red smoke and the sounds of DJ Calvin Harris mixing from the back of the bus was enough to wash away the disappointment of the night before. The LFC Women's Championship-winning squad was importantly in tow.

Jordan Henderson stated:

> We weren't quite sure what to expect when we came on the bus. Obviously [we are] disappointed with last night and how the season ended, but overall the lads have given everything and this is what it means to the fans. The least we can do is say thank you to them for what they gave to us this season, supporting us across the country, across Europe. To say thank you means a lot to the lads. We missed this a few years ago when we won the league, so to spend it with them now is really special.

Somewhere on the bus, Klopp drank in every second of the parade, in his sunglasses and backward-facing cap. He spoke to LFCTV onboard, looking both burnt out and jubilant at what he was seeing in front of him. His tone was one of sheer glee:

> In no club in the world could it happen that you lose a Champions League Final the night before, and people arrive here in the shape and mood that they are. It's absolutely outstanding.
>
> This is the best club in the world, I don't care what other people think. I was not sure what we can expect, we spoke about it before about what we have to do because we have to plan these kinds of things with our families. But I deeply hoped that we would find something like this. It's the biggest sign you can give to the rest of the world. Yes, we won two cup competitions, but we didn't win the last two.

More than the big-match wins and trophy lifts, Klopp's achievements can arguably be marked by moments like this. Just like that cold and dreary afternoon when they'd salvaged a draw against West Brom, Liverpool showed they would always be together. In a world of increasing confusion and division, that such a far-reaching entity could send such resounding messages of positivity, beyond the cold definitions of tangible success, was truly inspirational.

The city of Liverpool played its part in that. It had to show up for the team when it mattered, and it had to recognise that what the team was building with Klopp went further than results. It was created and nurtured over time. It was hope overcoming despair, and it was a message of unity and purpose its people were all too willing to embrace. It was Klopp, and they knew full well he understood them.

Chapter 15

Liverpool 2.0

NOT A great deal was known about Klopp's wife, Ulla, prior to 28 April 2022. The former social worker and teacher worked at a German school in Nairobi, Kenya for three years before meeting Jürgen when she was waitressing at his favourite bar in the western German city of Mainz. They would marry in December 2005. She later went on to write two children's books, in 2008 and 2010, the first of which had a football theme. She, like Klopp, become instantly at home on Liverpool's idyllic Formby coastline. They both regularly have family stay with them and their dog, Emma, who is notorious around the beaches and wooded areas of the village.

Ulla had generally remained out of the headlines at Liverpool, that was until news filtered through on 28 April 2022 that Klopp had signed an extended contract until 2026 and cited the influence and impact of his wife on the decision to stay put:

> The most important contract I signed in my life was the one with Ulla. That's where it started again. We sat in the kitchen at the table and Ulla said, 'I can't see us leaving in 2024,' and I was like, 'What?' That's how it all started, and when that started I thought, 'Let's have a think'. If she would say, 'Honestly, I love the football and I love watching it, but I actually want to go home,' then we would go, that's the truth. She started it and here we are.

Anxiety had been building on Merseyside from as early as the start of that season, with Klopp due to enter his penultimate campaign in 2022/23. Many couldn't comprehend the thought of his departure. This was, of course, testament to the culture the manager had built at the club that was now entirely consumed by his image and character. Klopp had led Liverpool through incredible highs and despairing lows. Throughout these adventures, people felt grateful for him and what he brought to the city. Nobody was ready for the journey to come to an end.

The notion of Klopp and his value to the city is felt well beyond its confines. It continues to be a relationship that broadcasts the wider ideology and values of Liverpool. That it can be seen as far afield as Australia and beyond remains one of its most impressive achievements, as Ben Chapman testifies:

> For me, I've found Jürgen's time at Liverpool captivating. He's box office. He's a manager, a coach, a politician, a father figure, a philosopher, at times a comedian and many more. But all under the title of Liverpool manager. Cool, calm and calculated but somehow always natural and emotional.
>
> As I've gotten older and learned more about the city, its values and politics, I've realised how they align with my own. The way [Klopp] has approached his role and carried himself in the job has made me proud that I'm a Red and Liverpool has never felt closer to Sydney. The term 'LFC family' gets thrown around a lot, but it has never felt truer under Klopp.
>
> Visiting the city, what I've gathered is that its people want to, and do, feel extremely close to the team and club, and want the club to represent them and who they are. Since Jürgen has been manager there's been a shift in how the team and club are portrayed to show a culture. I think it's great for the

club, who should be representing and championing who and what the city of Liverpool is. It's the identity of the football club and it's what sets them apart from other teams.

Klopp was quick to ensure that any decision to stay relied on the buy-in of both Lijnders and Krawietz, who also penned extensions on their current terms. The manager appeared amid increasing speculation that he was set to stay, via the club's official channels, serenading supporters with the words to his chant of 'I Feel Fine' – The Beatles' classic rewritten in homage.

The extension was celebrated at boardroom level, with FSG's Mike Gordon unable to hide his delight at the announcement:

> Jürgen wanting to make our future to be as bright as our present is a big statement. We cannot rest or consolidate. We have to think at all times about improvement and we are now able to do this in the knowledge that we have retained a manager who not only shares our vision and ambition, he remains determined to deliver on it. For these reasons and many more, it is beyond thrilling to know Jürgen Klopp will lead us into this new era.

The extension represented so much of Klopp's journey as manager of the club. He was the longest-serving Premier League manager and was on course to leave Liverpool having been in charge for over a decade. Liverpool have been able to boast financial stability and unimaginable success during his tenure. It's a long way from the battle at the High Court that stopped such a valued institution being liquified back in 2010.

Where Klopp now sits in relation to all-time great Liverpool managers is a topic of eternal debate. To many he will be their Dalglish, Paisley or Shankly thanks to the generation of success he's delivered after around two decades of relative scarcity. The comparison to Shankly is perhaps the most interesting. He was someone who not only ignited a football club but lit up an entire city and brought people together behind a cause they could relate to. That brings its own pressures, but as Karen Gill admits, some of the parallels are unmistakable:

> The comparisons I see between my granddad and Jürgen are mainly based on aspects of their personalities. My granddad was a very honest man and very fair. I get the impression that Klopp shares these qualities. There is a directness about them which can also be witty, especially in dealings with the press. I would also say that his relationship with and empathy towards the supporters reminds me of my granddad. They 'get each other'. They all share the same passion for football, almost to the point of obsession. Finally, there seems to be an affinity in terms of their socialist values and principles.

To say that Klopp simply 'understands' Liverpool without backing up what that means can make such a statement reductive. Lines can be written about him, as they were with Shankly, singing the virtues of how they were able to make the people happy. In truth, it's an ability to create a place in time. It's about parallel journeys and how a place evolves alongside a certain generational era of a football club. There are clear examples that demonstrate that the person in charge at Anfield really matters and makes the city a better place by his presence.

Since 2015, the city has experienced the national injury of Brexit, which has been compounded by incredible hardship and transition – most notably by a lack of vision and funding from central government mired with chaos and alleged criminality at council level. All of this topped off by a global pandemic. That's enough to test a city and its people to their limit. Liverpool needed a beacon of hope, which Klopp provided. Granted, there are large sections of Liverpool's Evertonian contingent who would have something to say about that. But beyond his political outlook or his pragmatic approach to world issues, this is in fact his greatest asset and gift to Reds in the city.

Atkinson suggests:

> I don't think there's a comparison in terms of giving life off the pitch since the 1960s. Not since Shankly built a team from the ground up has there been such a societal impact as this. The precursor for Klopp is 2013/14, which almost gave everyone a big practice run for what was to come. The city was insane. Every weekend was like St Patrick's Day.
>
> The question is: does Jürgen create something or does he fill the space created? Does he work out there's a space to be filled or does he do it accidentally and go from there? I think there's elements of pot A, pot B and pot C in this. The sporting influence is massive. There's a sentence a lot of people won't like, but a huge figure in Liverpool's history is Dejan Lovren. He plays a lot of games in the side which wins the league and is a massive factor in them reaching back-to-back Champions League finals as well as the run to a Europa League Final in Basel.
>
> The point is that Klopp at Liverpool has been really unorthodox and really incremental with the odd massive leap forward – such as selling Coutinho and buying Van Dijk, and suddenly you're stood in Shevchenko Park. I think he's understood where a quantum leap is possible on and off the pitch. He doesn't run on the pitch to grab Alisson [in the 2018/19 Anfield Merseyside derby] just because it's Everton; he does it because it's a building block to a team breaking 90 Premier League points. I'd like to know what he thought

was magic compared to what is in the plan. What was spontaneous and what was thought out. I hope we get to find out one day.

Thorp adds:

> Liverpool is a special place with a unique identity and outlook. It's a city that has been through a lot when you look at its treatment by governments both in the past and more recently, the fight for justice over Hillsborough and the dark days of deindustrialisation and decline. This has fostered a tough but caring mentality amongst many Scousers.
>
> I think Klopp totally gets this and he isn't afraid to speak his mind when it comes to social and political matters. Whether it is talking about the importance of the welfare state, concerns about Brexit or his worries about the rise of the far right, the manager has nailed his caring credentials to the mast, and I believe they chime very well with how many across the city of Liverpool feel. Klopp once said, 'If I am doing well, I want others to do well,' which I think sums up his stance pretty well. It is essentially about fairness and looking out for others – you can see why Liverpool fans love him so dearly. Of course, his incredible achievements on the pitch are a big part of this, but for most Reds it goes much further than that.

Liverpool found themselves in what Klopp has described as a new era: they have to climb the mountain again, and the perception was that Klopp would guide them. It's a process that hasn't happened overnight and it's taken some anguished setbacks to materialise. The 2022/23 season was one many would euphemistically call 'transitional'. The truth is Liverpool looked physically and mentally shattered for most of it. Legs and minds were getting older and burdened by the slog of a 63-match season in the previous campaign. A short summer break and World Cup crammed into the middle of it hardly helped either. The 2021/22 season came right off the back of the disappointment of another tantalisingly close quest for the title; with the expectation to go again and maintain the same level of performance, it was no wonder the players looked so flat. Supporters were also feeling the helpless frustration and baffling circumstances of how UEFA could allow what happened at the Stade de France to transpire.

Maintaining previous standards under such change was always going to prove difficult. It may be a simple case of an ageing squad unable to cover ground as easily as it once did, but it gradually felt that the team had to become something completely different and new. To the credit of everyone, the squad rallied towards the closing stages of the season, amassing 24 points from a possible 30. It wasn't enough for Champions League qualification, so the Europa League beckoned. From a campaign of such upheaval and transition, there was still obvious positives. Benfica forward Darwin Núñez had shown glimpses of mercurial brilliance. The emergence of Spanish youth prospect Stefan Bajčetić was an unexpected plus, and new January signing Cody Gakpo looked like another intelligent attacker who would only get better under Klopp.

Anfield still provided its moments. Despite frustrating performances (including a 5-2 collapse at home to Real Madrid that effectively dumped the Reds out of Europe), wins against Manchester City and the astonishing 7-0 demolition of United would go down in history. The United win was one that left both teams in complete shock. Erik ten Hag's United had been described as a 'tough bunch' by Gary Neville on Sky Sports earlier in the day, but fell apart so cravenly that captain Bruno Fernandes was remonstrating with his bench because he hadn't been substituted off late in the match.

Even for Klopp, who labelled it as a 'freak result' to accompany praise of a 'top performance' in his press conference, the sense of surprise was visible. Just like Ten Hag knew his name would always be over the door of such a result, Klopp will have been aware that in the mire of an underwhelming season, he and his team had just served up a classic forever etched in the history of English football's biggest fixture.

Klopp seemed determined and energised to oversee football operations and build a new team in his image. After a disappointing season, there was a feeling Liverpool could once again find their way to triumph over adversity. There was never a worry that a setback would cost the German his job. Liverpool had created a project, one everyone thought Klopp would be around until at least 2026 to oversee.

The summer of 2022 saw Mané depart for Bayern Munich in a move that many were surprised by. Liverpool decided to place their faith in Núñez, who had impressed (and scored) against them in the Champions League the season prior. By the time a truly underwhelming season had ended, Klopp was preparing for a midfield reshuffle. Milner, Keïta and Oxlade-Chamberlain all departed. Firmino finished his Liverpool career with a goal on his Anfield farewell against Aston Villa.

'Bobby' – as the smiling renegade with Brazilian flair and humble ingenuity was otherwise known – received a dazzling send-off weeks in the making. A player who epitomised so much of Klopp's first and best Liverpool team remained adored by the Kop. He stood tearfully gazing around Anfield, pondering over a glorious part of his life that was now over. Firmino should be remembered by Liverpool and English football as a player who redefined the position of striker and changed the club's fabled association with the number nine forever.

While his departure was scripted, there was one to come some weeks later that took everyone, including Klopp, by surprise.

Henderson's move to football's increasing wealth power hurt Liverpool and caused a divisive reaction. Fabinho also decided to move to Saudi Arabia, but his exit was slightly dimmed by the heat around the captain's decision and a truly awful season by the Brazilian's standards. Organisations such as Kop Outs were disappointed in Henderson's decision to force through a move to Al Ettifaq and join up with their new manager, Steven Gerrard.

There remains the argument that Firmino and Fabinho being waved off with a lionised goodbye while Henderson being a topical debate of morals and virtues among supporters may scream hypocrisy in itself to some. The reason Henderson was so topical was because Liverpool's captain had painted himself as an ally to inclusivity; he stood in unison with the LGBTQ+ community and its fight to be part of football without discrimination. Moving to a place that has an abhorrent human rights record around issues of sexuality painted him as a hypocrite. Others were mystified that he simply wouldn't want to continue the honour of being Liverpool captain for as long as he possibly could, given how he had to undertake his own road to perdition at Anfield just to be a Liverpool player. It must also be said there were those who simply didn't see any issue and were even sympathetic to his financial opportunism.

Either way, Klopp and Liverpool faced one of their most important summers in history. A fifth-place finish and a last-16 humbling at the hands of Real Madrid had left them out of the Champions League. There was also – what some quarters deemed – a failed sale attempt by FSG in November 2022. After creating a sales deck for prospective buyers and seemingly testing the appetite of those potentially willing to purchase the football club, anticipation for a potential sale quickly diminished. Briefings quickly shifted to a search for minority investment, which was found in September 2023 when a small stake of the club was sold to US private equity firm Dynasty Equity. It was mooted that the investment would cover any debt acquired from the Anfield Road reconstruction as well as outstanding transfer fees.

The summer's transfer business included recruiting a range of midfield recruits. Brighton's Alexis Mac Allister, Dominik Szoboszlai from RB Leipzig, Ryan Gravenberch from Bayern Munich, and Japan captain, Wataru Endō, from VfB Stuttgart all came in. This followed the protracted targeting of Moisés Caicedo and Southampton's Romeo Lavia, who both ended up signing for Chelsea.

Klopp was asked about the pursuit of Caicedo the morning it seemed Liverpool would land the 22-year-old Brighton midfielder. An apparent fee of around £115m was agreed. This left many pointing the finger at a manager who once publicly said he would never replicate United's then-world record €105m fee for Paul Pogba in August 2016. 'Everything changed. Do I like it? No. Did I realise I was wrong? Yes. That's the way it goes,' Klopp told reporters before facing Chelsea.

Transfer flux hasn't deterred Liverpool's mood or the undeniable sense of new identity to a team Klopp titled 'Liverpool reloaded', and which has also been dubbed 'Liverpool 2.0'. He now leads a team with a much younger average age who haven't had the physical and mental drain of persistently challenging at the very top.

Van Dijk and other members of the old guard remain, as does the manager and his coaching team, but the energy around the place and on the pitch is vastly different. Klopp feeds off such a buzz. He fosters unity via his team's performance, and that's still one of the defining features of the club and city. His latest contract was due to end in the summer of 2026, but many would have hoped his enthusiasm and energy towards Liverpool's latest incarnation would convince him to stay longer.

Klopp will always be led by his modesty and honesty. He has always maintained a stance of staying somewhere if he feels he's a positive force there. Once that changed, it was always likely he would change the situation rather than continue without the ability to bring every aspect of himself to the role. Whatever has transpired, he'll surely go on to be adored in the same way as Shankly and a select few icons.

'Will he go on to have a similar legacy [as Shankly]? Very possibly he will,' says Karen Gill. 'My granddad was manager for 15 years and managed to keep the support of the fans even in difficult times. In this new era of modern football that may be extremely difficult to achieve, but if anyone can, I believe Klopp can.'

Klopp has always presented a united front when faced with questions around transfer policy and the need to boost the squad. It remains his belief that there are times when certain players are not available or an inflated value isn't representative of talent. His authenticity has been questioned, but he's someone who craves cohesion and places trust in those around him. If any decision on transfer policy is made, it's usually made together.

There's another point, which the contents of this book allude to, about football's increasingly fraught relationship with money. Expenditure in the millions, even billions can be encouraged by people who themselves are essentially struggling to get by. Britain is in the grip of a financial crisis. Thousands of people in the UK are left to choose between eating or heating. Liverpool need to sign the best talent and retain their high-value players to stay competitive. Yet the discrepancy between money inside the stadium and out in the city once again shows that football remains a social outlier. Should that be the case? There is validity in the sense that football's entire platform provides escapism, regardless of social contradictions. We can look to Klopp and others to fall in line with working-class values, but, contrastingly, if we also encourage personal wealth and pursue FIFAnomics without ever consciously making the connection to the disparity between that and the situation around us, will anything change?

None of this is binary. Supporters of all backgrounds may see things differently based on their expectations. Some might have championed FSG's pursuit of higher ticket prices or Super League participation because it could mean being bigger players in the transfer market. Others would cite that such a pursuit is morally unacceptable but may still want the club to be both successful and representative. It's perhaps unfair to bring every fan's expectant need to Klopp's door. If football is merely an entertainment platform, Liverpool and Klopp have been box office for most of his tenure in charge. He has fulfilled the role and gone over and above in that sense.

Despite the morally uneven nature of football's trickle-down economics approach, Liverpool under Klopp have offered lessons in collective will that many have never experienced. To that end, L4 has become a corner of earth that has provided so much more than a glossy set-up at odds with its surroundings. If anything, somehow the Liverpool manager has managed to bring everything closer together.

MacCambridge says:

> He's my favourite coach ever, in any sport at any time. In the modern age, when managing a team is like being a CEO 24/7 and being responsible for everything – Klopp is the best I've ever seen at rolling with any of the myriad variables which comes a manager's way and taking them in his stride. So many coaches are locked into the next game; Klopp's genius is that he's excellent at that but also understands what the game means to the fans, how the game is playing out in the media and what the larger social issues of the day are. To do all those things superbly is rare.
>
> He's brought people together. So much was made about Anfield nights. I still remember Gerrard versus Olympiakos in 2004 and that cauldron in the stadium, but those moments were few and far between in the decade before and after. It was all

about the past. With so much myth and tradition surrounding the notion of Anfield as a fortress. The fact that Klopp came in and made it more of a cauldron and more of a fortress than it had ever been before, that is an accomplishment

To transcend this massive myth about its existence for decades and make it even better and culminate it in Dortmund, Barcelona and other things accomplished in a way that is still a palpable 12th man doesn't exist in the modern age. Every other thing could exist, but if Klopp wasn't the manager, it wouldn't be as good. FSG were important, Virgil van Dijk and Mohamed Salah were crucial, but without Klopp it doesn't all come together. The whole is greater than the sum of its parts; the players are good, the manager is good, and the crowd is loud, but on certain nights when all of that comes together it is a hellish place to play, and Jürgen Klopp made it that way.

This book has explored the impact of one man's influence on a football team and city, both of which are inherently complex and require an understanding which exceeds conventional footballing norms. Liverpool's history won't change – nor will its beauty, its undeniable charm or, at times, its complexity. It will evolve only through its people and its representative bodies. Klopp has shaped the texture of the place in a way that will come to be seen as yet another golden era. A time where men and women, young and old, were able to see themselves through the eyes of their football team and felt represented in the way they wanted.

Jordi Holden proclaims:

> It has given me memories that I will take to the grave with me. I've gathered tickets and programmes that

I will treasure. Klopp at Liverpool has given me the opportunity to go to places I never thought I would and meet so many different mates who I now see on a weekly basis. It has changed my life – to be truthfully honest – and has made me realise that going to the match is the best social activity that I could possibly do, and what I want to do for the rest of my life. Although it won't always be this rosy, the memories we can now look back on thanks to Klopp; Madrid, Barcelona, Qatar, [winning] the Premier League, to the less glamorous wins like Villa, Arsenal, Leicester away. It has all given me a sense of belonging.

Hopefully I see him one day so I can thank him.

Epilogue

'WHERE CAN we live but days?' In many ways, that Philip Larkin line perfectly encapsulates Jürgen Klopp's time at Liverpool. Klopp nurtured a body of work that was layered, meticulously planned even, yet still made everybody feel in the moment. He created a sense that life was about the here and now, which remained in keeping with his authenticity and decency.

On Friday, 26 January 2024, Klopp announced that he would leave Liverpool at the end of the season. It was a moment we will all remember – where we were, what we were doing. Knowing that life would never be the same. In some ways, we were all that little boy in 1974. When Bill Shankly's retirement is revealed to him by a roaming Tony Wilson in the city centre, all he can muster in disbelief is the phrase: 'You're having me on, aren't you?'

I was in the middle of a presentation in London, the place I'd moved to post-pandemic. I genuinely couldn't compose myself and had to make light of it to some very understanding community members.

My own journey arc during his tenure has changed dramatically. I was no longer living in Jürgen's Liverpool, from the heart of the city, as I'd done for the majority of his years. But, importantly, I never did feel removed from what he'd created. It reached out and embraced you wherever you were. I would still go home for matches to take my seat in the Kop. To see him, to see them. Importantly, to feel a sense of days. Days are where we live, Larkin's poem tells us. We'll have one today and one tomorrow – sometimes we're happy in them, but we're not always in control. The days of Klopp were lived in ways like no other. One day I'll fully return to Liverpool, for times that will be lived differently, because I will be different.

It's important to remember that Klopp, despite his remarkable achievements here, doesn't win every trophy every year at Liverpool. Plenty of managers win silverware without being Jürgen Klopp. So how can we evaluate this man's success in a way that tells the whole story? I think it's easy: Klopp and Liverpool created a sense of feeling. He made the means justify the ends – the process and the purpose genuinely mattered. Every day spent under Klopp was an exercise in the value we feel towards ourselves, our home and our football club.

Liverpool is a place and a club increasingly defined by its people. They can be those who fulfil crucial, custodial roles such as manager of Liverpool FC, local business owners such as Angela and Sally-Anne, and those who are shaping and improving the lives of young people like Earl and Nuh. A feeling of being propped up by skilled, honest and well-intentioned individuals working collectively to harness a sense of hope and community. That will ultimately be Klopp's legacy on the grandest of scales. His bequest as Liverpool manager is that he gave society, not just fans, pure belief. 'Anyone can have a good day,' Klopp told Raphael Honigstein in 2017, 'but you have to be able to perform on a bad day. That's what you live for as a sportsman. You have to put up a fight.' He took that will of the pitch and put it into the hearts and minds of millions.

The city is far from free of challenges. Almost nine years on from Klopp entering the club, a recent council meeting outlined the findings of a report written by Liverpool's public health director Matt Ashton. They looked at overall health trends in the city and the key takeaways showed that, heartbreakingly, Liverpool's infant mortality rate is higher than the national average: every year, 26 babies do not reach their first birthday.

The same report also found that, on current trends, the life expectancy of Liverpool women will go into reverse by 2040. As things stand, the number of people in Liverpool with major illness is also expected to increase by between 33,000 and 38,000 by 2040. Shelter has estimated that 1,078 people were homeless in Liverpool on any given night in 2022 – including 465 children.

That so much of the prosperity from 2015 has dwindled is heartbreaking. National austerity and policy incompetence continues to blight the city. Other places have experienced similar suffering, but it always seems to be the citizens themselves that bear the fullest brunt of Brexit, the pandemic and one farcical government to the next. Yet Liverpool remains able to marshal resolve at every turn. To do that it needs people willing to continually propel it; fortunately, its charm and beauty remain limitless – even on a bad day.

The city will move forward. Change is always inevitable, nothing else is permanent. We have to keep remembering that, as we navigate the future of places and people. Now there's an entire generation of people whose life has been joyously touched by Klopp and Liverpool. There are youngsters who know nothing else but him, and elders who thought they would never see something like him again.

Friendships have been formed, stories have been written and joy has been shared in the fabric of a place in time – stitches of what happened when Klopp was here, and how it will remain eternally unique to those who lived it. Because things move and turn with such a sleight of hand, memories very quickly become just that: a fleeting glance held in a second's thought. But eventually this all comes down to effect – how emotion and desire psychologically influence us. Stirring experiences and feelings usually tend to be more intense and long-lasting, and Klopp's Liverpool was a feeling like no other.

That feeling, to me, is of a man I feel overwhelmingly grateful for. A person who showed me more about unity, belief

EPILOGUE

and authenticity than the bulk of adult role models across my life. He'll forever be a whirlwind of light, warmth and fist-pumping energy; of nights out, love and loss, of being alive and genuinely inspired, sharing in an infinite community.

I think back to that day in time, driving home on a sunny October afternoon in 2015, of a glistening waterfront and the eternal optimism. The day it all began with everything in front of us. I think of how Jürgen Klopp and Liverpool was unlike anything I'd felt before. Those days will remain with me forever. Those days were lived.